Just Off Main Street

A Neighborhood Naturalist's Almanac

Written and Illustrated by
Steven Mulak

Text and illustrations copyright 2005 by Steven J. Mulak

Design by Chilton Creative, Rockport, Maine

Printed by Versa Press Inc., East Peoria, Illinois

5   4   3   2   1

ISBN 0-89272-664-4
Library of Congress Control Number: 2001012345

Down East Books
Camden, Maine
A division of Down East Enterprise, publisher of *Down East* magazine

To order a catalog or purchase a book, call 800-685-7962, or visit
www.downeastbooks.com

Dedication

My mother has never made a secret of the pride she has in her children. That pride has been a fuel in our lives, propelling us forward. It's true even now.

This one's for you, Mom.

Steven Mulak and his wife live in Chicopee, Massachusetts

Contents

Introduction

THE ETERNAL KINSHIP

> There have always been two major problems: man and man, and man and earth, his environment. Neither stands alone, and the false solutions always turn out to be the ones that ignore that eternal kinship.
>
> –Hal Borland, *Sundial of the Seasons*

The Northeast is more than a geographical region: it's a way of life that thrives on the changing seasons; it's a blending of rural and urban existence found nowhere else; it's an area steeped in history, to be sure, but it's also one of the first places on earth where man and nature manage to live side by side without one overwhelming the other. Our part of the world enjoys four distinct seasons: lush summers, wintry winters, springs that make a young man's fancy turn, and autumns that are the envy of the rest of the world. Living here is an ever-ongoing celebration of those seasons.

We are a heavily populated area, with a web of interstate highways connecting our cities. The complexion of the countryside is shifting from rural to suburban, a trend which shows no signs of abating. The suburbs are where civilization and nature meet. Those of us who make our homes just off Main Street sometimes pretend that we live unaffected by nature, yet it surrounds us and influences our lives constantly.

Our twenty-first-century view of the natural world is somewhat distorted by mankind's self-centered, value-based interpretation of nature. Man sees "good nature" and "bad nature:" crops and weeds, furbearers and vermin, beneficial insects and pests, productive timberlands and those grown to trash trees. Nature, of course, has no such view of the world. Weeds invade our suburban lawns, mice slip into our garages and cellars, deer browse on our foundation plantings, June bugs rap against the screens, and vacant lots grow to sumac and poplar in the figurative blink of an eye. Wildlife—that is, everything that grows or creeps or flies—won't stay wild; it shares the suburbs with us.

But in a world populated by humans, how much wildlife is enough? What is our suburban quota?

A family living on the third floor of an apartment might think we need more wildlife. They have a birdfeeder at their window ledge and enjoy watching the pigeons.

On the ground floor of the same apartment, a mother might not be so sure. Raccoons routinely tip over her trash cans, and she finds deer ticks on the kids after they've been playing outdoors.

A man whose cat was carried off by a coyote is sure there is too much wildlife around.

It's all a matter of perspective.

We don't want hornets building a nest on the back porch, and we don't want poison ivy in the vegetable garden. Rattlesnakes have a right to exist, but not on the school playground. No one wants to push any of these elements to extinction, but neither do reasonable people expect that civilization will make a space in its midst so that poison ivy can grow or venomous snakes can roam.

Some changes, seemingly for the good, produce unforeseen

results. People cheered at the return of the moose to southern New England. They forgot what inevitably happens when one steps onto a highway at night, as they are wont to do. How many moose should be permitted in a heavily populated state? There are those who can make convincing arguments that the correct number is zero.

Twenty years ago we were fascinated by the natural changes that brought Canada geese to the Northeast. Now, with their numbers despoiling reservoirs and soccer fields, we are actively trying to persuade the birds to move elsewhere.

During my boyhood in the 1950s, possums and raccoons were virtually unknown in suburbia. I believe it was a direct function of the lack of leash laws. Neighborhood dogs were everywhere, crowding schoolyards and playgrounds. Although those dogs created their own brand of neighborhood problem, nobody had a skunk camped out under their back porch, either. But Rover no longer earns his name the way he once did. The sudden invasion of so-called problem animals into the suburbs seems more than coincidentally linked to the emergence of leash laws that keep our dogs from roaming.

There is a disconnection from nature that affects us all, and it manifests itself in various ways. Massachusetts recently voted to end trapping. A referendum campaign was mounted that resonated with the animal lover in all of us. The battle cry was "Ban Cruel Traps!"

Wildlife managers are concerned with whole populations of animals, and their place in the environment. Ordinary people, like the third-floor family that thinks we need more wildlife, tend to identify with individual animals. When decisions are made and votes are cast, the blurring of the line between the two outlooks often spells disaster. The referendum passed overwhelmingly, and trapping ended.

The main beneficiary of the ban was the beaver population. Beavers, of course, build dams and flood surrounding low-lying areas. Sometimes that flooded land contains roads or septic systems or farm fields. In those areas, beavers are at war with the infrastructure of civilization, and it seems they are winning. Not that the state didn't have beaver problems before the trapping ban, but what we have now are beavers out of control.

I spoke to Peter Westover, a friend of mine who was the Director of Conservation for the town of Amherst.

"Amherst is mostly flat farmlands," he explained. "The beavers are trying to put us underwater. I spent a great deal of time going to the board of health on behalf of farmers. It was always beaver problems —flooded farmland, backed-up drainages. In every instance, we had to hire a commercial outfit to come in and do at the taxpayers' expense what trappers used to do for free. They'd live-trap the animals and euthanize them. Nobody was happy about that sort of development.

"The beaver population is still growing unchecked, and they're getting desperate. They ate all the aspen in town, then all the maple, then all the oaks. Now they're eating hemlock, so you know they're just about out of food."

"Don't beavers have a natural enemy that might control their population?" I asked Westover.

"That would be the wolf and the wolverine, and neither has made an appearance in Massachusetts in the last two centuries. As such, the beaver hasn't had any controlling factor on his population except trappers. Now, with trapping prohibited, that leaves the beaver to worry only about getting hit by a car.

"Their population density is such that I'm surprised a virus of some sort hasn't done them in. Other cases of animal overpopulation usually end up with a die-off due to some disease."

Somehow, that doesn't seem the sort of solution we should be hoping for.

How many beavers are too many? How many geese? How many moose? How much wildlife?

For the six-thousand-year history of civilization, mankind's progress was dependent on nature. We didn't worry how much was enough because we were a very real and integral part of it. People grew food and fibers and made things out of trees and animal skins in one form or another. But our agrarian society evolved into one where plastics have replaced wood and leather and wool. People are distrustful of any food that doesn't come from a store. We chase the winter chill by turning a dial rather than by throwing a chunk of wood into the stove. Technology has advanced so that even Mr. Fix-it types no longer understand how things work.

We tend to fear progress not because it is inherently evil, but because it destroys so much of what we love. Turn on the television. In the news studio the potted plants are plastic and the cloud-studded blue sky behind the weatherman is a projection. It seems the natural world is something that has to be conjured up. Part of the fallout from society's recent evolution is a disconnect from nature, and we all feel it. Nature has become an inconvenience.

Some people succumb to progress and live supercivilized existences insulated from any but the most urban of environments. Their lives are a series of denials that they are a part of nature. In our society, it's not hard to do.

Others revel in the idea that they are indeed nature's children. Fishing and hunting and gardening fill a need in this sort of person, and if outdoor types make more of their activities than seems justified it's because of the unspoken part—the part that makes them feel like a participant in nature.

There is a dichotomy defined by man's affect on nature and nature's inexorable pull on our society. The two often tug in opposing directions, but are inseparable and endlessly fascinating. Caught up in that tension are everyday occurrences that appear to be commonplace but are, in fact, extraordinary in their detail and beauty. Man and earth are bound together in an eternal kinship. If this book is about anything, it is the celebration of that dichotomy.

Chapter One

THE RENASCENCE OF LIFE

Chill darkness checks the slow awakening, but
another day starts the deliberate throb again, the
slight breath of change, the incredible, inevitable
renascence of life.

–Hal Borland, *Twelve Moons of the Year*

The new year has begun.

Not the contrived New Year that we celebrate on January 1, but the natural new year—the first day of spring—that usually passes unremarked. Astronomers calculate the exact moment when the earth's axis is at a ninety degree angle to the sun, and the radio announced that spring began at 2:33 this morning. The ancients weren't that technical, but they always knew the day of the vernal equinox and celebrated it accordingly. For an astronomical instant, the length of day and night are equal. From now until the summer solstice three months down the road, the days will continue to get longer.

We've been seeing signs of spring since the sap buckets were hung in late February. For a resident of the snowbelt, each sign was cause for a minor celebration.

Certainly, as with any cycle, there is no real beginning or ending to the earth's year. Spring follows winter, then becomes summer and eventually autumn, and the cycle continues with the rearrival of winter. If there is a beginning to that cycle, it is an artificial one created for the convenience of man-the-timekeeper. But if nature had a calendar, here is where it would begin: the vernal equinox—the first day of spring.

* * *

Winter sometimes equates with silence. As summer passes into autumn and the weather cools, the noisy scrapers and singers of the insect world become progressively still. November rains quiet the crisp rustle of October's fallen leaves. As the brooks freeze, the sound of running water abates until only the wind is left to whisper and sigh in the bare branches. Finally, with the first snowfall, the silence is complete. Indeed, after a powdery snow, the outdoors can seem like a soundproof room.

But March finally breaks the quiet. Not all at once, to be sure, but with the thaw comes the sound of nature's oldest lullaby—running water. Later, when the thaw gets a foothold, the spring frogs will be out of hibernation and sounding off wherever there are vernal pools, even when those pools are rimmed with ice. But for now, the trickle and gurgle of each fresh springlet is music to the ears of the winter weary. You might need rubber-bottomed boots to hear it, but it's there for the listening—a spring tonic for the ears.

On the river, mergansers show up as soon as the ice has begun to clear. Driving by, I pull over and dig out my binoculars from the glove compartment, because the birds are worth looking at. There must be some awakening going on under the surface to attract these fish-eating ducks. Most of the river is still sheeted with ice, but here, in an open stretch of dark water, they've gathered to dive and socialize. The elegant white-breasted drakes throw their heads back in a mating display to impress the flock's more subtly colored hens. The hens, for their part, seem unimpressed. These are American mergansers, sometimes called common mergansers, more often called shelldrakes or fish ducks. It is difficult to tell exactly how many there are; they spend more time underwater than above it, then pop back to the surface in a location far removed from where they first dived.

Their sleeker relatives, the misnamed red-breasted mergansers, favor salt water during the winter months. They aren't as gaudy of plumage as the Americans, but the drakes of both species have a mallard-green head and an incongruous, brilliant red bill.

All mergansers are voracious fish eaters and are the bane of hatchery men and fish farmers everywhere. As a duck hunter, I can report that none of them are very good to eat. Actually, they're so bad that there is a joke about their table qualities: "Cook 'em with a brick," goes the joke. "Then throw out the merganser and eat the brick."

During the winter, the river ice has alternately broken up and then refrozen after each spell of mild weather, so this thaw by itself carries little meaning. But the return of the mergansers is a definite sign of spring.

Another vernal signal is appearing along the road edge where I've parked the car to watch the mergansers. It's just a leafless branch with a handful of tiny bits of gray fuzz. If they first appeared six weeks from now, nobody would pay much attention to them—something as simple as these early pussy willows would be lost in the profusion of color that will accompany the arrival of May. But here on a March day, when the wind and temperature make it seem more like Christmas than Easter, the first pussy willows can be as lovely as all the May flowers put together.

They're just little gray fluffy things called catkins, not even a flower but just the sheath of one to come, a swollen bud with the protective scales fallen off. They're hardly beautiful; it's what they do for the soul that makes them so lovely.

You can find them growing by a roadside ditch or along a sandy brook or often on a sunny bank where nothing else seems to thrive. Sometimes, at this early point in the year, they are opening in spite of the snow and ice at their feet.

Cutting stems of pussy willows seems to affect the plant not at all. I brought some home from a local roadside and was naïvely careful to take every other stem so as not to damage the plant. Someone came along after me and cut those I had left, but the following spring the same bushes sent up a new profusion of pussy willows, and, if anything, they were more plentiful than ever.

Willows of all varieties are remarkably vigorous and grow in places that would rot the roots of more noble trees. If any of those stories about fence posts taking root are true, the posts must have been cut from willow. In one form or another, they appear in every state in the Union. When the days lengthen and the sap rises in February, willow branches turn a rich, lively yellow as a sign of approaching spring. Shortly thereafter, all the willow kin produce inconspicuous fuzzy florets that can easily be mistaken for those of the true pussy willow.

But pedigree hardly matters—they all have the same effect. As part of nature's plan that includes malicious March snowstorms that sink our hopes, the willows bring forth a humble little row of catkins that can somehow buoy them up again.

* * *

On this mid-March day, I'm in the woods with my young English setter, Nancy. She and I are getting in some training time on woodcock currently passing through southern New England on their migration northward. Nancy hasn't yet figured out that her master cannot use his nose—at least, not in any way remotely like she can. That conclusion, which all bird dogs reach sooner or later, is a major factor in the development of the relationship between dog and hunter.

Woodcock are upland gamebirds that look like beefed-up but short-legged sandpipers. They have a long bill that they use to probe for worms in the soft woodland soil. Some 90 percent of their diet consists of earthworms; the other 10 percent is made up of things they happen to find while probing for the first 90. As such, they are definitely not a bird of rocky or frozen ground—they will be found where the worms are. Today they're in the lowland woods.

Two factors make woodcock ideal for training a young dog: they'll hold still when approached, and they give off a huge amount of scent. All gamebirds have scent, of course, but woodcock apparently reek of it—even a puppy can't miss them. There's no shooting involved in spring training, just the pointing and flushing of these cooperative little birds.

Because they're so important to my dog-training activities, woodcock are the one bird whose spring migration I monitor closely. In this part of the world the main migration seems to show up around Saint Patrick's Day, and the birds are right on time this year. It's not the celebration of all things Irish that draws them northward, but rather the start of the spring thaw, which takes place about mid-March in southern New England. It almost seems the impatient birds push the thaw before them, and their northward migration is like a giant wave that contains all the woodcock in America. As the thaw takes hold, there is a week or two when the birds are crowded into the lowland woods, and during that time a bird-dog trainer might provide a year's worth of hunting experience to a puppy. Then, suddenly, the woodcock are gone, off chasing the thaw even farther to the north. A few breeding pairs remain in the local woodlands, but the bulk of the population pushes on for Quebec and the Canadian Maritimes.

All of that happens sometime between mid-March and early April, whenever the spring thaw occurs. But in late February, occasionally as much as a month ahead of the main migration, the woodcock kamikaze brigade arrives. They are a small group made up entirely of young male birds. They can be found in the winter woods, even if there's still a foot of snow on the ground. In their search for food, they seek out wet seeps where the surface may be muddy rather than frozen, or they seek the narrow strip on the sun-drenched south sides of rock walls where the reflected sunlight redoubles the warmth hitting the ground.

In February no sensible worm-eating bird would be in the north, but these are not sensible birds. In a best-case scenario, the weather cooperates and they have a leg-up on the other males on the breeding grounds. If the weather turns sour—as it often does— well, that's why they're the kamikaze brigade.

There's no reason to think that woodcock are unique; other species also have their kamikaze squads. We hear of western hummingbirds in Central Park at odd times of the year, or Louisiana pelicans in Narragansett Bay. A number of robins and mourning doves and even bluebirds winter in the north. A few years ago, a visiting winter flock of redpolls adopted my father's bird feeder and stayed on right through the summer. And there are always a few eiders that don't bother returning north and, instead, summer in Chatham Harbor like the Cape Cod tourists they are.

Admittedly, some of those oddballs are just plain lost, but others represent nature's high-risk ventures, the ones who explore new avenues, the ones who are in place to take advantage of a potential climate change, the insurance against the main population being wiped out. Unfortunately, they are also the expendable ones, and they are usually expended.

Ahead of me, my setter points as we're passing through an aspen grove. Although I can't see it, there's a woodcock sitting on the leached-out fallen leaves somewhere in front of Nancy. I look hard and after a search I spot not the bird, but its shiny-black eye. Once located, the rest of the mottled bird's contour becomes evident as it squats like a lump on the forest floor.

Other gamebirds—ruffed grouse and pheasants—will run at the approach of a bird dog or a predator. Pheasants have powerful legs built for running and use them at every opportunity. But running is not part of the woodcock's modus operandi. With its scrawny little legs, the woodcock trusts to its protective coloring as a first line of defense. The bird in front of me squats like a chicken brooding a nest and blends perfectly into the leaf litter on the forest floor. When I look away, it takes me a long moment to find it again.

The woodcock is camouflaged. Many creatures hide—that is, they conceal themselves behind bushes or beneath fallen leaves. But protective coloring is a mask that permits a creature to hide in plain sight. Trout, for example, make no attempt to hide but are nearly impossible to see in the water. Yet, out of it, they can be as beautiful as a rainbow. Their backs are reflectively colored and patterned to blend with the bottom as seen from above the surface. Snorklers, with their eyes beneath the surface, have no trouble spotting fish. It seems a logical conclusion that the trout's camouflage evolved to protect against predators that are out of the water rather than in it.

In the art of camouflage, background is everything. During the summer, moths spend the daylight hours resting on the sides of my house. The house is the color of vanilla ice cream, and the moths appear as unusual bits of tree bark and dead leaves. Had they chosen a tree trunk rather than my vinyl siding as a resting place, they would be invisible to predators.

There is a reverse-camouflage dynamic at work in the avian world. Because birds often feed in plain sight of their predators, the males of many species evolved a bright, colorful plumage in contrast to the female's duller shades. With other factors being equal, a predator coming across a pair of wood ducks, for example, will automatically go after the highly visible—and expendable— drake. In the reproductive scheme of things, males are a dime a dozen, while the female usually has a long-term role in the rearing of a family.

Animals have evolved behavior patterns that correspond to their natural coloration in their environment. Removed from that environment, their masking pattern no longer works. Even the woodcock—he of the perfect camouflage—will show up if the bird has chosen to sit in the wrong place. I've spotted them before the dogs could show me where they were, but it was always in a situation where beech leaves had fallen and carpeted the forest floor; the uniformly pale, leached-out non-color of the matted beech leaves made the woodcock stand out, a dark lump on an otherwise light background.

Although the tweedy browns and grays and blacks on the woodcock seem random, all woodcock are marked as identically as anything found in nature. The pattern varies little from bird to bird. It is a product of the evolutionary process. Something in this particular arrangement proved so superior that it enabled the woodcock that first wore it to out-survive and out-breed those with a different pattern. All animals—trout, moths, even the woodcock —evolved their distinctive patterns and behavior over time through a dynamic that is the ultimate example of trial and error.

The concept of evolution is mind-boggling. As much as I try, I can't digest the amount of time required for species to have mutated and evolved in their diversity. It is a compelling revelation that awes everyone who embraces it.

Evolution and extinction go hand in hand in nature's scheme. Man is rightfully ashamed of the part he played in certain extinctions—the passenger pigeon is just one infamous example— but nature has been running new species in and out since the beginning of time. Given the evolutionary scheme, natural extinctions are inevitable. The Labrador duck and the ivory-billed woodpecker, both now extinct, were never common. They seem to have faded away as part of a cycle that would have gone on even if Europeans had never discovered the American continent.

Nature's evolutionary adventures continue, and not always in a timeframe measured in ages and eons. Loosestrife—that magenta flowering weed that appears in wetlands during the summer—has moved in and taken over, yet it was unknown in the Northeast when I was a kid; a blight completely wiped out the American Chestnut in little more than a decade; ticks have become a common problem in the Northeast's woodlands in the past dozen years; mockingbirds and cardinals and house finches are relatively recent arrivals in this part of the world; black-backed gulls now threaten the dominance of the herring gull wherever gulls are common. Populations swell and shrink and sometimes disappear, and each action sets off a chain of reactions, some of which alter the environment in a way that can only be called "evolution."

The whole process continues relentlessly onward, sometimes just off Main Street. There is a male English sparrow at the neighborhood park that has a chocolate brown bib and facemask rather than the sparrow's standard-issue black. He's a mutant, carrying out one of nature's experiments. If that coloration somehow gives him an advantage over other males, he might be the start of a whole new line of English sparrows. Most likely not, but nature is constantly trying. There will always be mutations and mutants— some few with a more durable impact than most—and because of them, evolution will go on.

Beneath the aspens, Nancy continues to stand on point, but she rolls her eyes back toward me, wondering if I've forgotten about her. I walk forward and flush the woodcock. The bird flashes its robin-orange underbelly as it twitters into flight, somehow propelling itself straight upward until it has flying room above the branches. Woodcock react in weird and unpredictable ways. Sometimes they'll fly off directly as if they're headed out-of-state and need to get there soon. At other times, they'll do as this one does: the bird decides it must have been mistaken and descends back down through the treetops and lands just fifty yards ahead.

Since they're nocturnal birds, it is possible that when the dog finds a woodcock the bird is asleep. As such, a trainer is not only flushing the woodcock when he walks forward, he's also waking it up. I know I'm liable to do a few crazy things upon suddenly being awakened, so I can't blame a sleeping woodcock for the unpredictability of his flight pattern.

I direct young Nancy uphill, away from where the woodcock settled back in. The bird has done its part—it held still and played the role of the cooperative training assistant. This bird may be heading farther north tonight and might be in need of its sleep. I wish him well as we head away. Good help is hard to find, after all.

* * *

On a recent outing to the sportsman's club, I noticed a fallen yellow birch tree partially blocking the gravel entrance road. The few vehicles that travel the road have had to squeeze by the fallen tree. Today I have my chain saw in the truck, and I'll make my visit to the club a little more worthwhile by reducing the fallen tree to cordwood.

I'll admit it: I'm a firewood scrounge. It's getting late in the season, but this March birch might still be ready for the fireplace by next winter. It'll go into the wood crib behind the more seasoned cordwood.

The birch is sixteen inches in diameter at the base. As trees go, it's hardly big. It fell not from old age, but because it grew tall and slender in the woods and then was left exposed when a road was cut through a few years ago. In falling, its root system has lifted a disc of soil and rocks that looks like some huge opened umbrella laid aside to dry after a rain. Trees that start out and grow in the open take on a much more stocky structure, and become resistant to being blown down in a strong wind. This yellow birch succumbed to the wind, as do most forest trees once their sheltering neighbors are removed.

I mark off and cut the fallen trunk at twenty-inch intervals. I'm always surprised at how heavy fresh green wood is, and how much water it must contain. Just the difference in weight in firewood when green, then a year later when it is properly dried, is amazing. Today's yellow birch is all dead weight, and the twenty-inch sections are about all I can lift.

On the newly cut butt of the tree stump, the growth rings invite counting. The outermost five are widely spaced, indicating the accelerated growth that took place once the tree's neighbors were removed for the new road five years ago. The tree was fifty-odd years old when it fell—it's difficult to tell the exact age because the rings in the middle run together.

It's common knowledge that you can determine at least the rough age of a tree by the growth rings in the wood, since a living tree adds a new ring each year. What's less commonly known is that each year's ring reflects that season's distinctiveness. A long, mild winter followed by a dry summer produces a ring with certain characteristics, and a brief winter followed by a wet growing season produces a ring with a different set of particulars. Those differences are often so subtle as to be noticeable only through scientific examination, but each ring is distinctive. As such, the tree rings become something of a code that recounts the weather pattern through the life of the tree.

I'm no expert, but looking over the rings on the birch stump I can easily find 1981. That was the year an infestation of gypsy moths defoliated the forests of western Massachusetts during May and June. The 1981 ring is conspicuous as a very narrow band among others that seem normal. Such markers will be identifiable on every piece of wood that grew in this locale during that time period.

Using the growth-ring code of trees of different ages, scientists can overlap dates backward through time. For example, they would count back to the inner rings of today's yellow birch and find the ten-ring sequence produced in the 1960s. Then they'd take a walk to the clubhouse and examine the timbers used in the garage, which was built in 1971 using locally cut lumber. In the grain of those beams they would match that same 1960s pattern, then find the sequence from the previous fifty years. By overlapping that knowledge on some old beams in a barn or a historic building, they could count back and codify the pattern another one hundred years or so.

In that manner, scientists are able to splice together a chain of definitive dates spanning centuries. They are able to interpret the code in the wood used in ancient buildings and establish the exact year the timbers were cut. It's a process that enabled them to nail down the dates of Indian cliff dwellings in the Southwest, which predate Columbus by eight hundred years.

When I'm finished with the chain saw, the truck sits heavily on its rear springs and the tires nearly touch the top of the wheel wells. The cut-up birch totals perhaps a third of a cord, but I always overestimate. When split small and tightly stacked, all volumes seem to shrink.

Free wood? I bend and stretch and try to ease out the kink in my lower back, the result of working while bending over. The argument could be made that this wood was paid for in a currency much different from the folding money in my wallet. In truth, the whole firewood scrounging process is something of a hobby with me, one that extends all the way to remembering the specific tree as the chunks are burned in the fireplace a year later. The silvery, satin-like bark of the yellow birch will be reminder enough.
But it's hardly free.

* * *

March is about mud and flood. Up until the advent of asphalt roads a couple of generations ago, spring was synonymous with cars and wagons stuck in the mud. A few warm days can generate mud, and it doesn't seem to matter that it hasn't rained or snowed in weeks. Just why is that, you might wonder.

The reason you can't dig in your garden in January is because the soil is frozen. Actually, it's not the ground itself that is frozen solid but, rather, the moisture the garden earth contains. All soil holds moisture in some percentage, and once it freezes, the ground becomes rock hard. It rains during the winter—or the snow melts—and, although some of that precipitation runs off, much of the winter-generated water permeates the ground and freezes. Until the spring thaw, accumulated groundwater is locked up.

Once the frost is out of the ground—that is, once the ground temperature rises above freezing—water that built up over the winter starts to flow again, and we have songs about cars getting stuck in the mud and on the riverbank dreading the waters of March. Even in a relatively snowless winter, the rivers rise in March, so it can't all be from snowmelt upriver, as is the common wisdom. The same winter-trapped ground moisture that generates spring mud is part of the watershed, and once a winter's worth of frozen water thaws, the rivers naturally rise.

In this part of the world, the Chicopee, the Fort, and the Westfield Rivers all flow into the Connecticut. During March, silver maples stand knee-deep in high water all along the riverbanks. Because of high water in the Connecticut, the Fort, which is running high itself, cannot properly fall the last few feet it needs to empty. In the lowlands around the towns of Hadley and Amherst, the Fort River backs up and overflows its banks.

There is a golf course in Amherst that I used to belong to. It boasts of water in play on twelve of its eighteen holes. Unfortunately, that means there is no golfing in the early spring; the water at issue is the Fort River, and it annually floods out several of the fairways.

Antonio Carlos Jobim wrote a lively song entitled *The Waters of March*. It addresses the craziness of this time of year: the floodwaters and the mud, yes, but the song also speaks of the promise of spring.

That's March. It's a promise—an IOU—of the coming of spring. There are everywhere signs that the change of seasons has begun, but of those signs few are green. March is a purgatory to be endured, but one that brings a certainty of May's flowers. It is the renascence of life.

Chapter Two

THE FLOWER'S BEGINNINGS

There is April, in the swelling bud. There is
spring. There are the deep wonders of the season,
not in the flower but in the flower's beginnings.

–Hal Borland, *Sundial of the Seasons*

With apologies to the month of March, it's really April that "comes in like a lion and goes out like a lamb." April often begins with the last snowstorm of the year, but no matter what April Fools' Day may have been like, the month will end in full springtime and whatever April was trying to accomplish will have been completed. Wet spring, late spring, too early or too long a winter, it won't matter. By the time the calendar page is flipped over and May stares out at the world, everything will be caught up. April, for all its unpredictability, is predictable in that respect.

I'm out on the golf course today. For those of us who chase the little white ball, a short-sleeve day in April is something special. The ground may still be soggy, and the weathermen may predict a return to jacket-and-sweater temperatures by week's end, but today it's breezy and cool, and for the first time in five months I've rubbed on sunscreen and I'm out for a walk on the grass.

The first real day of spring is like a great stretch and yawn in the morning. All around the course, tree buds are opening and pollen is in the air. Pollen is as much a part of the season as blue skies and sunny days, although hardly as welcome. Here on the golf course there is a solitary white pine tree to the left of the green up ahead, and the effect of the breeze through the tree is reminiscent of a dusty rug being shaken out—a cloud of pollen emanates from the tree on each wind gust.

The inconspicuous blossoms of all pines are not intended to be fragrant or showy or to attract bees. Technically, they're not even flowers in the botanical definition of the word. Instead, pines produce male cones that act as airfoils to launch microspores of pollen into the air to drift and, with luck, bump into a receptor female cone—what we all recognize as a typical pine cone—on another pine some-where downwind.

Some trees—those with colorful or fragrant flowers—evolved a reproductive strategy that attracts insects to their blossoms. The insects accidentally carry the pollen on their bodies from one flower to another, and will inadvertently brush some of that reproductive dust against the receptor of another plant's flowers. That strategy is rife with risk: without bugs at blossoming time, pollination can't occur. A too-cold or too-rainy spring that keeps bees inactive when the apple trees are in bloom spells disaster for orchard growers. All plants that are insect dependent run a similar reproductive risk.

The pines elected to go with a birds-and-bees strategy that bypasses the birds and the bees altogether. As I said, they depend on the breeze to carry their pollen. Because wind-borne cross-pollination is an indiscriminate hit-or-miss process (with the percentages heavily favoring miss,) a huge number of individual pollen grains must be released by each tree. For once, the quantity billions is not an exaggeration; thus, the haze of pollen on these springtime days

The pines produce the earliest of several waves of pollen. The oaks follow suit in early May, and during the growing season plants as varied as ragweed, corn, hickory trees, and ordinary lawn grass will be responsible for the runny eyes and stuffy noses of hay fever sufferers.

This morning, both the exterior and the dashboard of my truck were lightly coated with fine golden dust from pines in the neighborhood. Pollen must contain some sort of efficient adhesive because, once settled, it won't be blown away. It remained in place on the hood of the truck even after a half hour at highway speed.

Most organic material will decompose in a short period, but pollen is all but indestructible. It's found in peat bogs, where it was laid down during the last ice age, and it is still viable. Scientists study it and can determine the makeup of the forests existing at that time. Pollen is amazing stuff.

The midday shadows around the golf course are still long, but now they are on green grass. As such, they have abandoned their winter inkiness and seem to take on the color of the sky overhead. The grass has nearly grown out of its winter sere on many of the fairways, but the greenest places on the course are near the wet areas. The ground is soggy along the water hazards, where turtles are sunning themselves on rocks and logs, and grackles and red-wings populate the tangles of reeds and cattails.

There are bluebirds investigating the nest boxes that have been placed as 150-yard markers. On a sunny day such as this the males appear stunningly vibrant, the color of manganese blue right out of the tube. Killdeer alternately race-walk along the fairways, then proudly pause, as if showing off their exemplary posture. They'll occasionally take flight, calling their name in a high-pitched scream as they wheel and turn and return to earth like one of the balsa-wood windup airplanes I flew when I was a kid. Somewhere out in the bordering woods, a woodpecker hammers out a staccato riff, apparently auditioning for a part in the percussion section of the coming songbird chorus.

A woodchuck, unnaturally skinny after a winter's hibernation, is investigating the green shoots along the cart path. The before-and-after photos featured in diet ads have nothing on the wood-chuck. He'll triple his weight before October, then lose it all again over the winter. Right now there is daylight under his belly as he walks the weedy edge, and he looks more like a prairie dog than the badger-like creature he'll round into by midsummer.

Nobody golfs very well in April, at least not in New England. The winter layoff has seen to that. In truth, I'm not much of a golfer no matter what time of year it is: I'm usually too busy watching the swallows or looking for trout lilies in the wood edges to pay attention to where the ball went. Golf is fun, but three-putts don't bother me as much as they do my more serious golfing partners. The killdeer and the woodchucks don't seem to mind, either.

* * *

The first woodland wildflowers are in bloom now in an annual but very limited engagement. Beneath the leaf-barren birches the white blossoms of bloodroot appear like scattered bits of tissue above the forest floor. In the litter beneath the pines are the some-times-white, sometimes-lavender, sometimes-pink hepatica, as delicate as the African violets my wife pampers on the window ledge at home. The delicate blossoms of wood anemone and arbutus are worth seeking out, if you can find them. They are not nearly as common as they ought to be.

In the low areas, if you're not afraid to get your feet wet, you may find my personal favorites, the Jack-in-the-pulpit and the butter-cup-yellow marsh marigolds growing in and around running water. And, as if to offset the rarity of anemone and arbutus, there are the violets—blue, purple, white, with variations that seem infinite.

Woodland wildflowers are mostly bulb-type plants, springing anew from roots that lay dormant through the winter. The only sun available to them on the forest floor is in early spring before the woodlands leaf out. To take advantage of it, they get going as soon as the frost is out of the ground. These first flowers are short-lived blossoms, taking the sun while they can and often fading before the plant sends up its first leaf. Perhaps it is for this reason that nearly all of the flowers that man has taken into his garden trace their origins to the blossoms of the field rather than the forest.

In a few weeks—once the trees leaf out—the shade-loving spring flowers will make their appearance: Canada mayflower, Solomon's seal, (both true and false) starflower, trillium, and the impossibly delicate lady slippers. Those are all part of the second act of the woodland flower show, and it waits until the forest shade is established.

March and April can seem the tired part of the winter-to-spring transition. The mantle of snow no longer covers the damage of winter, and we all feel an impatience as nature pauses before beginning her spring cleaning. In the woodlands, early spring's first blossoms belie that pause. They're not as showy as a pasture grown to daisies and black-eyed Susans, nor as fragrant as milkweed or wild roses, but those come later, when the world is green and the sun is high. At this impatient time, the pure whiteness of a blood-root flower is a signal that spring at least has its foot in the door.

* * *

Here, in mid-April, migrant birds are returning in full force. Some have been making appearances in the neighborhood during the last half of March, particularly the grackles, whose rusty-hinge call is an irritating, if welcome, sign of spring. The few mourning doves and robins that hung around all winter were seen and erroneously reported as new arrivals, but now the real migrants are back in abundance.

The true insect eaters—the vireos and warblers and orioles—will wait another month or so, but they'll be along in due time. Right now, it's enough to hear a robin calling from the telephone wires. The robin, though not our national bird (he is honored as the state bird of three states) is the unofficial national symbol of spring-time. Robins are truly cosmopolitan birds, equally at home in the countryside, the woodland, or the suburban yard just off Main Street. Spring cannot officially begin until my mother-in-law has seen a robin strutting on her lawn.

The male robin's familiar song of repeated liquid phrases and pauses is a standard to which other birds are compared. That halting song has been translated as *Cheer-up, cheerily, cheer-up, cheerily*, but every robin seems to have a bit of the jazz musician in him. Each adds his own interpretation to the song that is "basic robin," and no two are exactly alike.

The robin is a member of the thrush family. That makes him a close cousin to the hermit and wood thrushes, to the veery and, though it seems incongruous, to the bluebird. As a card-carrying thrush, he is less an exclusive bug eater and more an omnivore, able to adjust his diet to whatever is available. Indeed, a noncon-formist branch of the robin family has given up on the migration idea and spends the winter in New England, usually near a source of winter fare.

The early colonists were ignorant of the robin's family ties to the thrushes and instead labeled him after the altogether different European bird of the same name. The orangey brown breast of our local bird reminded the homesick settlers of the smaller robin red-breast they remembered from England, and thus a thrush became a robin.

Birds have begun singing here in April, but that is only a part of a whole array of breeding-bird behaviors. Yesterday I saw a nuthatch doing a sweeping dance with a bug in its beak. He appeared to be using the bug to sweep the roof and the nearby environs of one of the backyard birdhouses. For a nuthatch, that's the avian equivalent of sending a dozen roses to the cute divorcée down the street, so this morning I'm doing what I should have done in February—I'm cleaning out the three birdhouses in the yard. Nuthatches nested in one of the boxes last year, and the very same bug sweeper I saw yesterday might have brought in the accumulation of twigs and grass I'm removing today.

Bird boxes have to be maintained. Mine have a drop-front design to make emptying easier. Squirrels occasionally try to chew their way in by enlarging the opening, and on a couple of the houses I have had to mount a second piece of wood to cover the enlarged hole. I drill one-and-one-quarter-inch entry holes to encourage wrens, but my boxes also host nuthatches and chickadees.

I've often thought it would be fun to put bands on the baby birds so when they later appeared at the feeder we might identify individuals as "one of ours." In *A Sand County Almanac*, Aldo Leopold writes of tracking a particular chickadee by that method, but the practice is illegal, at least for the casual purpose I intend.

When my daughters were little, they enjoyed the birdhouse cleaning, mostly because I'd invariably evict a family of mice that had moved in since the birds vacated the place the previous summer. The scampering mice would always titillate the little girls, and their shrieks were never those of fright.

One of my then-young daughters once asked, "Daddy, when will the wrens be back?" We had spent the previous spring watching the comings and goings of a pair of house wrens as they raised a brood in the birdhouse close to the back deck, and I knew she was looking forward to a replay.

"In May," was my initial reply, but then I added, "As soon as there's something for them to eat."

The obviousness of that answer can't be overstated. Insectivores eat insects—many exclusively so—and until those bugs come out in abundance, migration is a risky endeavor. For that reason alone, the return of the true insectivores is not so much a sign of spring but of summer.

An April snowstorm will doom all such migrants in its path. Non-migrating chickadees survive an entire winter's worth of bad weather, but they eat weed seeds and insect eggs and quickly figure out where to find both no matter what the weather. But migrating birds that are on an insects-only diet will die when they're caught in a spring snowstorm. They arrive emaciated from a long flight on which there is no coasting. They are in no condition to endure even a few days of starvation. A warbler needs to eat half of its weight in live bugs every day, something that can't be done in a snowstorm. Even simple cold weather will send insects back into dormancy.

In such a situation, birds die. People who should know better assume that migrating songbirds simply turn around and go south again if the weather turns bad. Humans would do that, but humans also make decisions based on information rather than primordial urges. Birds are not migrating because they've thought it over and have given the idea careful consideration. No. Instead, they're answering impulses we can't imagine. To think that a wren or an oriole can countermand those urges is wishful thinking. The bird doesn't realize the weather is warmer five hundred miles to the south. He doesn't even know why he is flying north, only that he must.

As if unpredictable weather isn't dangerous enough, the migration itself is a killer. Just the act of flying from wintering grounds to breeding grounds extracts a sizable toll on every migrating population. Most birds need to feed heavily before undertaking such a journey. They don't just put on some extra flab but actually double their weight. They need to eat heavily, and their migrations are often timed to the cyclic availability of high-octane foods. Something as bizarre as the amount of horseshoe-crab eggs in the Delaware Bay can have a profound effect on certain migrating shorebirds. When, for one reason or another, there aren't enough crab eggs for the migrants to beef-up, their numbers on the breeding grounds fall dramatically. All the birds start the migration, but many don't show up for muster at the other end.

During my career at sea, I spent eleven years on routes that crisscrossed the Gulf of Mexico. Sometimes during migrations literally hundreds of songbirds would land on the ship. Many rested and flew on, but others were completely exhausted. There would be warblers or thrushes or vireos all over the deck, most too weak to do more than hop a few steps at the approach of a human. Kindly sailors would put out bread crusts and pans of fresh water for the birds, but inevitably the deck would be littered with dead ones in the morning. It was evident that had the ship not been passing by, those birds would have fallen into the sea and become fish food. No one knows what percentage of a migrant population succumbs. The flight across the Gulf is clearly one of the factors that contribute to the adage, "Only the strongest survive."

Once, we docked in Corpus Christi, Texas, on a beautiful April Fools' Day. When I went ashore, there were small iridescent-blue birds everywhere. They had brownish wings and finch-like ivory bills and looked like the pictures of indigo buntings I recalled from bird books. But I had never seen an indigo bunting in the flesh. I assumed they were scarce. Since these birds were everywhere, they couldn't possibly be the rare indigo bunting—they had to be a species native to the area—or so I thought.

It wasn't until I returned to the ship and took out my field guide that I verified what I had seen. The book showed date lines to delineate the general migration progress of various species, and in the case of the indigo bunting the dotted line that represented April 1 ran right through Corpus Christi. It seems that indigo buntings migrate in a tidal wave similar to the woodcock, and I happened to be in the right spot on the day that particular wave crested on the Texas coast. I've never seen another indigo bunting since that long-ago April 1. On that one day I must have used up my lifetime's quota of sightings.

Of those years I spent in the Gulf of Mexico, we often unwittingly gave cattle egrets a ride from Florida to Texas. They would fly out to the ship as we passed close to the coast. All through the westward leg of the voyage they could be seen alternately circling the ship then resting on the railings, always looking forward as if offering advice on navigation. They'd finally go their own way once we were in the Houston ship channel. Another time we had a roseate spoonbill make the return trip with us, and that strangest of birds flew off toward land as we passed the Florida Keys, almost as if he knew where he was heading. Somewhere, some birder was marveling that these birds were capable of nonstop flight across the Gulf, never imagining they had simply stuck out their thumb and hitched a ride.

Once, in Valdez, Alaska, we inadvertently captured a crow among the garbage cans on the ship's fantail. Alaskan crows are smaller than those in the Northeast, but their habits are the same. Flocks of them would hang out on the stern, scavenging scraps and handouts the whole time we were in port. We were at sea when the trapped bird was discovered and released. Anyone who tells you birds have a built-in navigation system should have been there: we were only a half-hour out of Hinchenbrook and the Alaska coastline was still visible to the east, but that crow took off in the opposite direction, heading for Japan—four thousand miles away. I watched him until he was out of sight, and he flew due west "straight as the crow flies." He may still be flying for all I know.

* * *

In early spring, the flowing waters of the Northeast are high and swift and turbid, but now in mid-April things have returned to normal. The tops of the boulders have emerged from the streams and the water has become transparent again. It's fishing season.

Or, more accurately, it's trout season.

Trout—the beautiful native brook trout, the subtly colored naturalized brown, and the flashy hatchery-raised rainbow—are the fish of New England's woodland brooks and rocky rivers. In this part of the world, they seldom weigh more than a pound, and a sixteen-inch trout is a monster.

Springtime seems made for trout fishing. Trout live year round in the flowing waters of the Northeast, where they eat bugs in every shape and form. When the water is winter-cold the fish aren't very active and are rarely hungry. During the summer, when the water warms and the flow becomes sluggish, so too do the fish. They're still there in the deep holes behind the boulders and in the shadows of the undercut stream banks, but except for brief periods of activity at dusk and dawn, they snooze away the summer months in pretty much the same lazy way as people would like to.

But trout become invigorated in the spring. Once the March floods subside, aquatic insect life becomes active again, and trout follow suit. Trout fishermen emerge on the same schedule as the first of the streamside leaves and blossoms.

This is stream fishing. There are no boats involved, no outboard motors. Instead the trout fisherman pulls on his rubber waders and goes into the water with the fish.

For most anglers, the sport is replete with traditions, the most ironbound of which is that trout are caught on *flies.* All trout flies are visual lures and have to be seen by the trout. Thus, they need clear water to be effective. April is too early for dry flies that float on the surface and imitate newly hatched flying insects. Better to start with wet flies that match emerging insects on their way to the surface, or nymphs that represent the larva stage of various aquatic bugs. Some anglers favor underwater streamers that mimic swimming minnows. The river's drag on the line adds several degrees of difficulty to fishing a fly properly. Then there's the fact that the fisherman can't actually see the underwater fly in action. It's entirely a matter of feel. And magic.

There's a different world below the water's surface. Things are going on underwater that we cannot see or hear or take part in. Standing in the brook we are connected to it only by the feel of a piece of gossamer line. We throw our fly off into that other dimension, and a creature that neither breathes nor walks nor in any way resembles us finds it. We haul that creature from its world into ours, and are never quite sure of what we've got until we bring it to the net. It's magic. What else could you call it?

Are there fish here?

The mystery stated in that single question is behind the allure of stream fishing for so many of its devotees. A fisherman can't actually see the trout. Sometimes there is a swirl or a rise that indicates the presence of a fish moving below the reflective surface, but mostly a fisherman measures the chances of a trout being present by his understanding of the water and the surrounding environment. He operates on knowledge and a sizable ration of faith and hope.

While bass can be as subtle as a howitzer blast, to catch a trout a man must act like a trout. The fish are secretive and move without disturbing their surroundings. They create neither noise nor waves. They rarely reveal their presence.

So it is that the trout fisherman skulks along in the shadows, trying to be invisible to his quarry. He believes that if he makes a perfect cast to the spot where a fish should be, the trout will oblige him by being hungry enough to take his lure. And so he casts and strips-in his line and mends the slack as the currents too swiftly draw the line away from the drift he had planned. Then, he casts again. He ignores the fact that one of the definitions of insanity is to continue to repeat an action and expect a different result. Instead, he likes to think of fishing as a victory of hope over experience.

Sometimes trout will eat june bugs or wasps that fall into the water, or they will rise to a stray fallen bit of leaf. That trout are routinely caught on worms speaks volumes to the idea that they are always discerning eaters. Fishermen sometimes have success with flies that resemble bumblebees or caterpillars, or with strange fuzzy patterns that imitate nothing at all.

But that's only sometimes.

At other times, trout can be very discerning and will dine actively, albeit selectively, on only one particular insect that happens to be hatching along the brook. It might be stoneflies or mayflies or something almost too small to be seen, but the trout won't eat anything else no matter how appealing it might appear. In their fishy way of thinking, it seems that once they've figured out that this particular bug can be eaten, they don't want to figure out anything else.

At such times fishermen try to "match the hatch." From the assortment of flies each fisherman carries with him, the right size and color and pattern is selected. To fool a selective trout, it must be a perfect match to the particular flying insect that is emerging and flying low over the water. The fly is tied on and presented to the feeding trout. The trout rises to the perfect imitation and strikes. The hook is set and the line plays out. The trout tries to swim toward the shelter of a snag or some rocks. If that happens, the delicate filament of leader will break and the fish will be lost. The fisherman tries to exert the right amount of pressure on the fish— enough tension to keep him from gaining the shelter of the underwater tangle, but not so much that he breaks the fragile line.

Sometimes the fisherman brings the trout to hand, and sometimes his touch isn't subtle enough and the fish snaps the leader or the hook pulls out. No matter, he has matched the hatch, and for a brief instant the fisherman has entered nirvana. He has outsmarted a fish with a brain the size of a garden pea.

At least, that's the way it's supposed to work.

In truth, the fisherman rarely has the right match. Oh, he has a dozen of everything else known to mankind, but for some reason he doesn't have the right one.

Or, if he does, on his back cast he hooks an overhanging alder bush, then spends the next ten minutes sloshing around in the shallows trying to unhook and untangle his line.

Or, with all else going as planned, by the time he reels in and changes tippets and ties on the exact right fly, the hatch is over and the fish have returned to contemplating the virtues of fasting. Sometimes these trout-feeding frenzies only last as long as the hatch, which can be over in ten minutes.

Oh, I almost forgot: Sometimes the man catches the trout. Some men actually go fishing to catch fish. But for most anglers—I plead guilty to being one of them—fishing is an excuse to participate in nature. I'm out on the water not just to witness what's going on, but to be part of it. I am a predator, albeit a benevolent one since most of the fish I catch are released back into the stream. But as I wade, I am as much a part of the April morning on the brook as the song sparrows in the alders and the trout lilies nodding their yellow heads in the shade beneath the hemlocks.

There are early frogs and a few turtles at the water's edge, and wood thrushes and brown thrashers that somehow hop in the shallows without making a splash. And then there are the fisherman's rivals: kingfishers work the brook, rattling a strange chuckling call as they dart from bare branch to dead snag in roller-coaster flight. Sometimes, unnoticed in his statue-like stillness, a great blue heron waits in the shallows. When startled, it takes flight with restrained power and the awkward grace of a lawn chair being unfolded.

And, of course, there's the river itself; if a man aspires to be a fisherman, he'd better like water. He feels the gravel bottom and the chill of the river that hugs his boots tightly to his legs. He leans into the push of the current. Immersed in the river, he is a part of its goings-on. There are reflections and currents and distortions in the transparent water and the enchantment of bubbles rising from the depths to be swept away by the current. They are the same thing that fascinated us all as little boys, and their fascination hasn't dimmed with the passing of time.

The trout, when they're there and when they're cooperating,

are a necessary part of the equation. But they're not all that trout fishing is about. Men are out on the brooks in April because they need to be, and the trout are only an excuse for being there.

Chapter Three

BLOSSOMING AND THE BUZZING BEES

May is . . . change and growth, blossoming and
the buzzing bees, birdsong everywhere; sunlight
and replenishing rain. It is life after dormancy,
irrepressible life

–Hal Borland, *Twelve Moons of the Year*

It's a telling comment on our love affair with spring that we name baby girls after the months of that season: *April, May, June.* Springtime has a corner on our affections. It is a love affair, and we've waited all winter for this time of year. Every spring day is reason enough for rejoicing.

Just off Main Street, the chartreuse season is beginning. Along the roadsides and in woodlands and front yards throughout the suburbs, new leaves are popping out on the trees. Those new leaves are not yet pumped full of the chlorophyll that will power them through the growing season, and their green is a pale, grayish version of their summer richness. From a distance, the tiny new leaves of every spring tree form a nimbus around the branches, and their summer contour becomes obvious, a chartreuse artist's sketch to be fleshed out later. The pin oak on my front lawn is opening its buds, and the dainty leaves that emerge are in their exactness reminiscent of a newborn baby's hand. They are fully formed in every detail, a miniature version of June's mature leaf.

I am never more aware of how many cherry trees there are at the roadside and in the wood edges until they come to bloom here in early May, with blunted plumes of lacy white flowers at each newly leafed branch tip. There are pin cherries and chokecherries that never amount to much of a tree, and our native black cherry that often does. The webworms that some call tent caterpillars love cherry trees of all kinds. They feast on the newly emerging leaves, and are busy now making their gossamer nests in the crotches of the tree's branches.

Also coming to bloom are the apples. There is no mistaking the wild crabs that dot field margins and open areas, because they crowd their blossoms so tightly on each branch they seem to be the ruffled sleeve of a girl's white satin dress. I'm not so sure that the tradition of a bride wearing a white gown didn't spring from the May loveliness of an apple tree dressed in white blossom, a promise of the coming season of fruitfulness and plenty.

We had a gnarled old apple tree in the yard of our previous home in Wilbraham. Although it wasn't much for producing fruit and could look downright scary in the wintertime, each May it was glorious with white blossoms. Individually, apple blossoms don't smell like anything at all, but a tree full of them has a light fragrance that, if you could bottle it as perfume, would hint of blue skies and gentle breezes and cool spring days during the chartreuse season.

* * *

In May, unless you spend the month indoors with the windows closed, you will hear the songbirds earning their title. No matter where you live, birds sing during every hour of daylight, but particularly at dawn and through the first hours of early morning. Just as we can walk by something for years without pausing to truly look at it, so too can we hear birdsong all our lives and never really learn to digest what it is we're hearing.

When Hollywood needs a nonexotic birdcall, they almost always imitate the cardinal or the robin for their soundtrack. Among songbirds, the clear whistle of the cardinal and the repeated, paired-note cadence of the robin are arguably the most easily recognized birdsongs in America.

As I sit this May morning on the screen porch with my coffee, there's a tiny song sparrow in the basswood tree, waiting his turn at the feeder. He's going to eat some of my sunflower seeds, and while he waits he sings for his breakfast. I'm certain that I'm getting the better of the deal. This sparrow's song seems to have been composed by Liszt, or at least inspired by the same virtuoso, show-offy impulse. The sparrow lifts his head and effortlessly produces an andante riff that varies between sweet and stunning with enough arpeggios to make Liszt proud.

The goldfinches that have been visiting the thistle-seed feeder all winter now offer repayment, too. They sing constantly and only pause long enough to fight with one another. Their piccololike song is as simple and lovely as a melody by Satie.

House wrens, busy near their nest in the backyard birdhouse, sing a hurried, bubbling call reminiscent of a Chopin impromptu. The white-throated sparrow also pays homage to Chopin, but he favors some of the simpler études. In woods behind the house, the plaintive contralto of the hermit thrush might have been scripted by Debussy in one of his more pensive moods. Warblers, with their myriad brief songs, are somehow reminiscent of whistled melodies set to the rhythm of an old-time sewing machine, and vireos seem to echo bits and pieces of the warblers' songs from their lofty perches in the forest canopy. Towhees, if you're lucky enough to have them near your backyard, burble the most cheerful of whistles, and in the blossoming oaks the oriole's clear, liquid song seems something a flutist might play on a bubbling water pipe.

On the back fence the mockingbird sits alert, doing "covers" of all the avian hit tunes, and the catbirds in the shrubbery offer their own jesting imitations of what they hear, seeming to laugh up their sleeves all the while. And, of course, the cardinal's loud whistle and the robin's familiar halting mazurka-like cadence are welcome additions to the songbird chorus.

Are they all singing out of joy as they seem to be, or is there something more to it? As a duck hunter who knows a little about calling waterfowl, I can tell you that mallards say a lot more than "quack." Like all ducks, they make different noises to communicate with one another. Duck callers imitate the greeting call and the lonesome hen call and feeding chatter and a dozen other signals in the language that is basic mallard. Crows talk to each other with meaningful variations on the common "caw," and turkeys have a language of at least a dozen calls. It's not much of a stretch to imagine that other birds possess similar communication skills, and that birdsong, lovely as it is, actually contains a message.

Almost as proof of that assumption, a wren flits up onto a branch and sings a brief riff outside the birdhouse. The song is evidently a signal to his mate inside, one that says, "I'm here to relieve you." The inside wren pops out and flies off, and the singer goes in to take over brooding duties.

The song sparrow near my screen porch has sung all winter long, but it has been a quiet warble, almost the sort you might sing to yourself. Now it's May, the breeding season, and the bird's song becomes clamorous as he sings for the pure joy of it.

Or, at least it seems so.

In truth, nature has far more important intentions than just pleasing humans. There are complicated reasons for bird song, all of them bound up with breeding ritual, courtship, and territorial claims. Although the experts can't agree on the "whys" of bird-song, it is a fact that most birds quiet down as soon as their eggs hatch and there are mouths to feed.

So the song sparrow probably isn't singing to make me happy. But, it's May, the sparrow sings, and I'm happy nevertheless. As I said, I'm certain that I'm getting the better of the deal.

* * *

We listen to a song—in this case, one sung by a bird—and then try to put words to it. It is part of human nature, because we have trouble remembering tunes unless they have words to accompany them. Bernie Taupin made a career out of writing lyrics to Elton John's music, and Hal David scripted the poetry that we sing to Burt Bacharach's catchy songs.

But lyrics were never put to any of Chopin's lovely melodies. (*Always Chasing Rainbows* is the one exception.) It's not that people didn't try—his piano melodies just defy verbalization. And it doesn't work for birdsong, either. There is a basic impossibility in converting noises into words and warbled whistles into phonics. Such attempts might come under the heading of onomatopoeic transcriptions, but I wouldn't presume to use that term in conversation.

Oh, some birds seem to be saying something when they call. Bobwhite quail and killdeer and phoebes were all named for the calls they make—or at least what we hear when they're calling. The chickadee has an onomatopoeic name, also; it actually sings *Chick-a-dee-dee-dee*. There was a whippoorwill that spent several nights in the woods behind my house last summer, incessantly repeating his name until it became the sole reason we shut the windows and turned up the stereo.

But mostly we interpret what we hear. The blue jay that screams "Thief! Thief!" in the backyard does not yell "Voleur! Voleur!" when he's in French-speaking Quebec. He's not actually saying something—or if he is, it certainly isn't in English. The fact that we can't agree on what sound a dog makes just underlines this fact. Does Rover say "Woof?" Or is it "Ruff?" Or perhaps "Arf?"

But we have given words to birdcalls, nonetheless. My Uncle Hank once told me you could recognize the ovenbird's call because he says, *Teacher, teacher, teacher!* When I listened, I discovered he was right.

But it's a one-way street, a way of describing a call you already know. The articulate essayist Robert Finch observed that putting words to birdcalls gives "a sense of them to the ear remembering how they sounded." There aren't many birdcalls that could be recognized by the human words assigned to them. It's hard to imagine an uninitiated listener reading that a white-throated sparrow sings *Poor-Sam-Peabody,* and then, hearing that bird's five-note whistled call while on a walk in the park, equating it with the written description.

Maybe the *Konk-ler-REE* call of the redwing blackbird is one of the few birdsongs that someone might recognize just by its phonetic spelling, and the *Wichity-wichity-wichity* of the common yellowthroat might pass muster, too. But the towhee song is written as, *Drink your TEA!* and the call of a bluebill is supposedly its formal name of *scaup,* but I've never been able to equate those lyrics to what I hear. The human voice seems to follow the same sound pattern as a meadowlark's call when we speak *Spring-o'-the-year,* but that's a stretch. Some interpretations, particularly those attributed to vireos and warblers, are ludicrous. And, I'm sorry, but goldfinches do not say *Po-tato-chips.*

I admit that my hearing is in decline, and I'm sure that for the past few years I've missed the subtle high notes. I used to hear waxwings before I'd see them. They appear unexpectedly, always in small flocks, chatting constantly as they work a wild apple tree. For reasons unknown, French Canadians call them chardonnay. One field guide describes the waxwing's call as a "high, thin lisp." Evidently, it is in an auditory range that I can no longer hear, because it seems those chattering birds are a lot quieter these days.

* * *

There was an eclipse of the moon yesterday. They occur about twice a year. People in Africa and India were able to see the eclipse during their nighttime hours, but the moon was not in the sky on this side of the world when it happened. High-school science teaches us that in an eclipse situation, the moon passes through the shadow being thrown by the earth. But in looking at the illustration in a science book, it's hard to understand how the moon ever misses the earth's shadow—the earth is so much bigger than the moon, after all.

It's a matter of distance. The earth is three and one-half times the size of the moon. That ratio is about the same as a basketball is to a baseball. That doesn't surprise too many people—it's shown fairly accurately in science books' illustrations. But what books can't depict—what everyone has trouble believing—is that the two balls would be twenty-four feet apart. By the same scale, the sun would be eighty-eight feet across and a mile and three-quarters away. When it comes to astronomy, the distances are always beyond our comprehension and are truly astronomical.

Each time the moon passes behind the earth in its monthly rotation, there's a chance it might cross the earth's shadow. But the moon's orbit is not in the exact same plane as the earth's path around the sun, so the moon misses the shadow on most of its revolutions—remember they're twenty-four feet apart. But sometimes, as was the case yesterday, the moon's path takes it right through the earth's shadow and we have a lunar eclipse. It lasts for a few hours and can be seen by everyone on the side of the world that is experiencing night. Sometimes sunlight is refracted as it leaks through the earth's atmosphere and slightly illuminates the shadowed moon with a dull coppery red light, but in truth an eclipse of the moon is not at all spectacular.

But an eclipse of the sun is.

I saw one when I was a young man on the tanker *Esso Gettysburg* in the spring of 1970. We had delivered a load of heating oil to New Haven, Connecticut, and had left port that morning on our way back to Texas. It was March 7, the day of a solar eclipse on the East Coast. On the radio, the news was full of that story.

Unfortunately for New Yorkers, in astronomical terms they were just a whisker west of the shadow's path, and all anyone in the city saw was a singularly unspectacular partial eclipse. Everyone dismissed all the hoopla that had preceded the event as so much overstated hokey.

But the path of the total eclipse passed over the Atlantic about sixty miles east of New York City, and for a minute or two the shadow fell on the *Esso Gettysburg.* As the sun was gradually covered by the new moon, shadows appeared to double as if coming from multiple light sources. The day became progressively darker and then, at the moment of totality, it was as if someone had switched the lights off. The sky was still blue, so the darkness didn't resemble night, but it was as dim as it gets after sundown on a clear day.

The bridge deck of a tanker in ballast is eighty feet or so above the surface of the water, so on a calm day it's possible to see about twelve miles in any direction. During the eclipse, I could see sunlit water a few miles away all around us, yet it was twilight-dark on the spot where we were. It was a remarkable experience. The total eclipse lasted less than a minute, and the whole thing didn't take a quarter hour from start to finish. What I saw on that bright, clear day on the Atlantic was the most spectacular celestial event I ever hope to witness.

For such a solar eclipse to take place, the moon has to be in its "new" phase. As such, the moon is in the daylight sky all day long but goes unseen because its dark side is facing the earth. Since both the sun and the moon are the same relative size in the sky, during an eclipse there is a brief time when the new moon blocks out the sun completely.

Even though the moon is twenty-two hundred miles in diameter, the huge size of the sun causes the moon's shadow to be cone shaped. The narrow end is the part that reaches the earth during an eclipse. Its width depends on how far the moon is from the earth and what part of the earth is struck by the shadow—the earth is a round ball, remember. In the exact path of the shadow, the eclipse is total. From everywhere else it's a partial eclipse with the new moon blocking some of the sun as it passes in front of it, as was the case in New York City in 1970. Anyone who saw that eclipse from dry land can tell you that with even with a tiny bit of sun peaking around the disk of the new moon, the effect isn't in the same spectacular lights-out category as a total eclipse.

We can't forecast tomorrow's weather with any amount of accuracy, but we're somehow able to predict all the details of astronomical events—including every eclipse—with uncanny precision. People think astronomers spend their time looking through telescopes, but their real work involves sophisticated mathematics. The size and path of the shadow that one moving globe will cast upon another one hundred years into the future requires calculations that boggle the mind; they make the quadratic equations we all struggled with in high-school algebra seem like tic-tac-toe.

There will be other eclipses. The moon passing through the earth's shadow, if unspectacular, is at least a phenomenon to take notice of. But if you ever have a chance to witness an eclipse of the sun, even if means traveling to a far distant place, I'll guarantee that you won't be disappointed.

These cool days in mid-May are routinely wonderful: the constant birdsong of the returning migrants, the fragrance of lilacs and apple blossoms, the world-at-large coming to leaf and flower. May days are full of blossoming and the buzzing bees, and are such that sometimes we can't seem to let them go, even when they turn into moonlit May evenings, with or without an eclipse.

Chapter Four

THE QUIET ABUNDANCE

... Every field, every roadside, every woodland
and meadow is evidence of the quiet abundance
with which the earth clothes itself year after year.
No matter what man may be doing, the
fundamental earth is not a hostile place.

–Hal Borland, *Twelve Moons of the Year*

It's June, and I'm out investigating the possibility that I might beat the birds to the wild strawberry crop later this month. In the meadow, down among the low-growing strawberries, Deptford pinks are in bloom. They're a small flower, only a half inch across, and grow in clumps and patches mixed in with the wild grasses of field margins. Their color is as close to Day-Glo pink as you'll find in nature.

Hal Borland made an issue of the idea that the color pink was named after the botanical name given to this class of flowers. That is, the color was named such because it resembled the flower, not the other way around. That was news to me, and at first it seemed a bit of a stretch.

Then I realized that the pastel purple color we call lavender is named after the flower of the same name. Pastel orange is peach because it resembles the fruit. Purple is synonymous with violet; again, the flower gave its name to the color rather than the other way around. Light brown is called tan because it is the color of tanned leather. Maybe the most famous case of an object lending its name to a color is orange, named centuries ago in France after the mispronunciation of the French word for the newly imported citrus fruit.

Pinks by any other name would be just as lovely, and I snip a fistful to bring home to Susan, knowing that even a large arrangement will fit in a champagne flute.

Wildflowers add color and grace to the outdoor world from the time the first dandelions appear in March until the hard frosts finally kill the last of the asters in late October. At one time or another, we've all succumbed to the temptation to pluck a few flowers. It doesn't always work out as we had planned, and as often as not we're disappointed in the results once we get them home. I wouldn't rush to the assumption that anyone would make the same mistakes with wildflowers that I have.

Among the questions that need to be answered before picking any wildflower are, *Is the plant endangered?* One such threatened flower is the fringed gentian. They appear in fields like miniature blue violet tulips, so intensely colored that it seems they might stain your clothes. If and when you find them, they will be in groups that appear to belie their scarcity. They're tempting, but you should pass them by, as well as any other unusual wildflower you're unsure of.

Will picking the flower damage the plant? For almost anything that grows in the woods, the answer is yes. That means do not pick lady slippers or jack-in-the-pulpits, the two that are most tempting.

On the other hand, daylilies propagate chiefly through extensions of their bulbous roots, so the flowers are all but superfluous to the well-being of the plant. If the plant is a woody bush, such as pussy willows and wild roses and mountain laurel, you won't hurt anything by cutting a few stems.

Annuals are a different story. Picking *all* the flowers from an annual means that that particular plant cannot reproduce. Be sure there are some flowers left to produce next year's seed, if not on a particular plant, at least on others nearby. That said, cutting an armload of stems in a field of goldenrod is not going to effect next year's production—that is, unless you mow the entire field.

Many wildflowers are like delicate inflated balloons with no rigidity of their own, held erect by slight internal pressure. The living plant produces that pressure through capillary action, which means the flower becomes a punctured balloon as soon as it is picked and wilts almost as quickly. Roselike mallows with their almost crepe-paper petals are a good example of a wildflower that will wilt before you can get them home, and sometimes even before you can get back into the car. The species called bouncing bet has the same reaction, as does Indian pipe.

Then you should ask yourself, *Do you really want them?* Few flowers will look as glorious in the house as they do afield. An example is red clover, showy and eye-catching against the dark green backdrop at the roadside, but puny and pathetic when arranged in a vase. The same is true of campions and buttercups and a lot of other small but lovely wildflowers.

In every instance, the domestic flowers that we plant and cultivate trace their origins to a wildflower somewhere in the world. In some cases, as with mountain laurel, it's simply a matter of giving the wild plant fertilizer and room to grow, then enjoying the flowers it produces. The evening primrose of borders and flower beds is obviously not far removed from the weed of the same name that grows at roadsides and is sometimes pulled out of the very garden where its cultivated cousin is being pampered. Similarly, gardeners selectively bred the familiar butter-and-eggs to arrive at the plant we know as the snapdragon—the flowers themselves are identical. Pansies and Johnny-jump-ups and violas all trace their origins to the common wild violets that grow everywhere in the Northeast. Daisies, sunflowers, and asters are only slightly changed from the area's common wildflowers.

The beautiful hybrid tea roses that my father grows in his garden are descended from the same wild roses that are now coming into bloom in June. My father's roses need more pampering than a whole family of spoiled children, and almost without exception they hardly smell like roses at all. One whiff of June's wild-rose fragrance makes it easy to understand that when man first brought roses into his garden, it was for their scent rather than their looks. Wild roses smell absolutely wonderful, never cloy-sweet. The fragrance that carries and drifts on the June breeze has to be the loveliest in the out-of-doors, bar none.

All wild roses have simple flowers with just five petals. If the blossom has more than five, the rose is not wild. The flowers of the rugosa rose—sometimes called beach rose or sea rose—are the deep pink color we've named rose. (Another case of a flower lending its name to a color.) The rugosa is the one with the big, fleshy rose hips, the wrinkled foliage, and the so-spiny-they're-almost-hairy stems. There are several other varieties of wild rose that can be found in sunny locales. Their first names are as varied as Virginia, sweetbriar, dog, swamp, and pasture. Each is a small, low-growing shrubby vine with pale pink five-pedaled flowers, and each blossom produces that same delicate rose fragrance.

But for a visual display, no rose is more spectacular than the all-white multiflora, blooming now as generously as the apples did a month ago. It is found almost everywhere and has become an unwanted invasive plant in many places. It often takes over old pastures and abandoned orchards, forming continuous impenetrable thickets. In its favor are its abundant, berry-like fruits—every outdoorsman I know calls them thornberries. They are a staple in the diet of grouse and dozens of other birds. As a cut flower, multiflora doesn't last long, and the petals fall in just a few days. When you cut an armload for their beauty and fragrance, you'd better wear gloves and a long-sleeved shirt—like all roses, the multiflora is serious about its thorns.

Nature produces flowers to attract insects that will pollinate the plant. When we pause to enjoy their loveliness, we should remember that pines and grasses and a lot of other plants manage the same reproductive task without flowers at all. Wildflowers, like butterflies and autumn leaves and birdsong and so many other things in nature, are unnecessarily beautiful. Nature didn't have human appreciation in mind when flowers evolved their myriad shapes and colors, but that doesn't mean we should appreciate them any less. In June, a field grown to black-eyed Susans can startle and delight the senses.

Be startled. Be delighted.

And be thankful.

* * *

Over the June meadow there are dozens of dragonflies working in the sunlight. They hover, then dash sideways to catch flying insects. Dragonflies might be the most successful experiment that nature ever undertook. They are hardly changed from the three-hundred-million-year-old fossils found in coal seams. Those drag-onflies, like today's, made their living by hovering and dashing to catch bugs on the wing.

When I was a little boy I used to shoot at dragonflies with a BB gun. (If you have to ask why, you've never been a little boy with a BB gun.) The BB's speed when shot from an air rifle is slow enough so that the shooter can actually see the pellet flying toward the target. As such, I could often see that I had made an accurate shot, but somehow the dragonfly, with its unfocused compound eye, could identify the speeding BB. Those dragonflies from my youth never dodged in panic but were as casual as a matador stepping out of the way of a charging bull. They would move a little higher or lower and let the flying BB pass. I don't believe I ever hit one in an entire boyhood of trying.

That story might serve to explain why I routinely find butterflies in the grill of my truck, but rarely a dragonfly. They have a predator's vision for motion, and a predator's reaction to it.

Summer is about bugs. In my own take on the entire invertebrate world, there is a continental divide that separates all bugs into two distinct categories: those that bite and sting, and everything else. I am very concerned with mosquitoes and blackflies and hornets and especially with horseflies, but I have nothing against any of the other bug-like creatures that populate the warmer months. I know Japanese beetles think the leaves on my back-yard linden tree are candy, and, as grubs, they have similar thoughts about the roots of my lawn, but just so long as they're not biting me they're okay in my world.

Entomologists argue about such things, but their varying estimates put the number of insect species in North America somewhere around ninety thousand. In any given acre of meadow in June, there are more bugs alive than there are people on earth. That's a scary thought. It seems evident that in the ecological war that is constantly being waged on the earth, it's the plant kingdom versus the insects, with each continually evolving in an attempt to outmaneuver the other. In that ongoing drama, birds and mammals and people are just bit players. Bugs rule.

* * *

One of our favorite vacation destinations in June is Acadia National Park on the coast of Maine. Unlike other parks that are built around a single outstanding natural feature, Acadia is a piece of the ordinary—a chunk of the Maine coastline—set aside in its wild state and immune from future development. Of course, there are those of us who think the entire Maine coastline is extraordinary and who wish it could be preserved in its entirety. The rocky coast of Maine is rife with jaw-dropping beauty, and in Acadia it is accessible to anyone willing to put on hiking shoes and take a walk.

"Down east" is the vernacular label for the Maine coastline, specifically the area beyond Ellsworth. Driving U.S. Route 1 to Acadia, the compass in the truck rarely strays far from the "E." Maine is north of the rest of the nation, but getting there involves a lot more "E" than "N."

The down east climate is different from that of the rest of New England. The breeze off the ocean and the geographic reality of being situated at the same latitude as Lake Superior means the weather is decidedly cool. In mid-June, apple trees and lilacs are still flowering in Maine. Springtime arrives two weeks later than in the rest of the Northeast, and at the other end of the season, autumn arrives two weeks earlier. A couple weeks at each end may not seem like a big abbreviation, but they translate into a very short summer that's over before it really gets started. In my books, when I write that spring is in full flower all through the Northeast by the end of April, my Maine friends write notes in the books' margins to the effect that they wish it were so on the coast of Maine.

For the artist in me, vacations are always about painting. I can think of far worse ways to spend a summer than taking a random right-hand turn off U.S. Route 1 and portraying whatever ocean scene I find at the end of the side road. On the Maine coast, every new vista is a painting. Boats are the obvious subject matter of countless pictures, but the real artistic draw is the interaction of sea and rocks, and the coast of Maine has an abundance of each. The truth of the matter is that painting is the excuse I use to spend a few hours in fascination, watching the ocean.

At the south end of Acadia is an ocean view within easy walking distance of a parking lot. There is a light breeze, enough to keep the insects away. (Outdoor oil paintings done on calm days always have a few tiny bugs stuck to the canvas. I'm certain they're suicidal art critics, intent on a final statement of disappointment with my efforts.)

The tide is just beginning to fall as my sketch takes shape. I'll have to compensate for the expansion of the rocky shore as the water recedes. In this painting, the center of interest will be the surf smashing against a few offshore rocks. The foreground is a jumble of boulders.

From a distance, the granite appears to be a delicate shade of pink. Up close, however, it's coarsely speckled with flecks of dark gray, white, and brick red. It's an illusion—no solid-pink color could shimmer as Maine granite does. In painting, that trick is called broken color. The Romantic-era painter Delacroix made the trick famous, and the Impressionists played it and played it and played it. Later, Seurat and the pointillists exploited the trick and made it the centerpiece of their style.

As difficult as it is to imagine, granite was formed deep below the earth's crust. The geological explanation is that the molten rock cooled very slowly—perhaps over a period of centuries—and the minerals contained in the molten mass formed into comparatively large crystals as they slowly solidified. The speckles that define granite are those actual crystals; the white is quartz, the dark shiny stuff is mica schist, and the brick-colored rock is feldspar. In other granites, the feldspar is gray or brown, depending on impurities within the mineral itself. The dark gray granite of western Massachusetts has a very fine salt-and-pepper grain, indicating that the molten rock solidified more quickly than this coarse-grained pink granite here on the Maine coast.

On the canvas, my granite is formed with terra rosa and zinc white, and shadowed with manganese violet. Pink rocks and an active gray green sea under a sapphire blue sky—the scene can only be the Maine coast.

There are graceful gulls and terns wheeling over the breakers as I paint. In a song from the 1960s, Judy Collins sang of birds "stitching to the sea the sky," and I always imagined it so since I first heard that line. In my seascapes, I always place a bird on the horizon as a unifying element, and if the bird seems to be stitching the line of the sea to the sky, so much the better.

Less graceful are the few eider ducks just beyond the surf line. Most eiders are breeding in the Arctic at this time of year, but these malingerers must be of a different persuasion. They fly the way I swim—with a panicky wingbeat, almost as if they're afraid of falling. Like all ocean ducks, they seem uncomfortable in the air and are much more at ease on the water.

There are other small black seabirds with bright red bills and white wings. They circle crazily off the water and seem to routinely crash into the bordering cliffs at Otter Point. I later learn they are properly called guillemots and have nests on the cliff face. They must do some tricky aerial maneuvering as they land at their nests, but to my eye they fly like novice pilots without learners' permits.

After a couple of hours, the light has changed and warmed as morning becomes midday, and the falling tide has exposed so many new rocks that the scene is becoming unrecognizable from the one I sketched just two hours ago. But all is not lost: the painting is blocked in and the shadow pattern established; the canvas needs only an hour's worth of detail to be completed. I took photos when I started, and I'll later use them to finish this scene in my studio at home.

Tides are amazing. The engineer in me can't be convinced that, over time, the working of the tides wouldn't slow down the earth's rotation. No matter how slight, the drag of the tides is not counteracted by another force. There is a disconnect there somewhere, because the tides have been rising and falling for a few billion years and if they've had any effect at all, it hasn't shown up yet. As with so many other of nature's great questions, we can postulate, but definitive answers are as rare as finding a buffalo nickel in your change.

* * *

The summer atmosphere is often hazy, and stars don't appear as bright in the night sky as they do at other times of the year. At home, even on an exceptionally clear summer night when the stars are out, so are the mosquitoes, and that's reason enough why stargazing isn't high on my list of activities on a warm evening.

All of which makes a clear and breezy June night on the Maine coast a pleasure of the rarest kind. Over the beach, the sky seems a great inverted bowl. The tide is approaching high, and the waves break rhythmically on the sand and rocks, filling the air with the sounds of the world's oldest lullaby. It's well after 10 P.M. before the sky becomes its deepest midnight blue, and the dark clarity goes all the way to the horizon. The stars are vivid pinpoints in the clear night air. A walk under the moonless sky, with the cool ocean breeze keeping the bugs at bay, is irresistible.

The constellations to the north are familiar, although their position in the sky at this time of year seems to be inverted, with the Big Dipper to the left of the polestar. Navigating around the night sky becomes a matter of recognizing the brightest stars. High in the east there is the "summer triangle" made by three brilliant white stars: Deneb, Vega, and Altair. Hercules is the constellation straight overhead, and the curved handle of the Big Dipper seems to point toward the brightest star in the western sky, Arcturus.

But tonight, as clear and dark as it is, the overriding aspect of the night sky is the hazy irregular ribbon of light that starts at the southern horizon and pours across the eastern half of the sky to touch the horizon again in the north. It's the Milky Way, never a more prominent feature than during the summer months. On a moonless night such as this, it seems to be a glowing cloud.

The Milky Way is the galaxy we live in. It is shaped in a great flattened swirl much like the symbol for a hurricane used on weather maps. The sun and the earth and the rest of our solar system are located out in one of the swirl's arms.

In summer, the earth's position is such that the night sky faces directly into the dazzling center of our galaxy, and the bright gauzy band of light that is those billions of stars is the sort of thing they name candy bars after. During winter, the earth's night side faces outward through the spiral arm, and the part of the Milky Way that we see at that time of year is narrower and not quite as dominant.

Unless you live well away from suburban streetlights, your view of the night sky isn't as clear as it might be. Growing up in the suburbs, I was a teenager before I saw the Milky Way for the first time. As a kid I was interested in everything, including astronomy, so I had read about the Milky Way and had thought I'd seen it from the backyard on clear nights. Then we went on a family fishing trip to Maine north of Moosehead Lake. The nearest electric light was sixty miles away. What I saw then in the unpolluted Maine night sky convinced me I had been mistaken—up until then, I hadn't seen anything.

Light pollution is a twentieth-century phenomenon. The millions of streetlamps and neon signs light up the night atmosphere and prevent us from seeing the stars. It's a bit like looking through a layer of cheesecloth. The more lights there are around you, the more pronounced is the obscuring cheesecloth effect. Prior to the advent of the electric light, nobody had to be told that the Milky Way existed—it was an obvious and integral part of the night sky, and could be seen just as well from Main Street as from Moosehead Lake.

Of that Maine trip, I recall my brother and I canoeing on the quiet lake after a day's fishing. As it grew dark and the stars emerged and threw their reflections into the still water all around us, the three-dimensional effect was such that we might have been paddling through the cosmos. It was an overwhelming experience, one not easily forgotten. The artist within me would like to capture the effect. It would take a very big painting.

Monet painted wall-sized images of water lilies and reflections on the water and mounted them in a circular room in Orangerie,

France. He wanted to capture the sensation of a summer's day by the Oriental water garden at his home in Giverny.

It didn't work for Monet—his paintings are lovely, but they're paintings, after all. Visual impressions work, but in this case the impression is so much more than visual. There is an eternal rhythm to the outdoors, particularly in June, and sometimes we need to close our eyes to feel again the ethereal summer breeze and the grass beneath our feet or the night air as we canoe through the cosmos —or as we walk the beach at Otter Point.

Chapter Five

A BLIND DATE WITH SUMMER

July is hot afternoons and sultry nights and
mornings when it's a joy just to be alive. July is
a picnic and a red canoe and a sunburned neck and
a softball game and ice tinkling in a tall glass.
July is a blind date with summer.

–Hal Borland, *Sundial of the Seasons*

There is a painting by Monet that I have long admired. It is entitled *The Broadmore Oak,* and it depicts a massive old oak tree growing at the edge of a forest. Monet delicately portrayed dappled sunlight on the tree trunks and the forest floor, yet he showed the oak in all it's gnarled, monstrous beauty.

Today, in an imitation of Monet, I'm off to do a painting that I'll call *The Cady Street Elm.* I'll try to use the same subtle color scheme to create a similar effect, but painters only do imitations of Monet, and the result is never to be mistaken for the genuine article.

Equally distinctive are American elms—they can not mistaken for other trees. As they mature, their shape is unique and their curvilinear branch structure is vinelike and without angles. They reach ever higher with their leaf-bearing branches, and the overall impression is that of a tall vase overflowing with foliage. The leafy twigs that droop like tendrils from the canopy only add to the effect. If a tree can be elegant, elms are.

As lawn trees, maples and beeches and lindens tend to spread out low to the ground and produce a shade so dense that grass can't grow beneath them. From a distance, if you look into a maple in full leaf on any summer day you'll find that the interior seems to be black—not simply darkened, but immersed in shade so dense it appears black.

In contrast, elms grow tall and umbrella-like, and it was their open airiness that once made them the shade tree of choice. They were favorites for city planting. Every town had an Elm Street—the name became synonymous with Anyplace, USA. On tree belts and city parks, the elms grew into immense giants. Then, during the 1940s and 1950s, Dutch elm disease (a fungus) began killing mature trees, and cities with extensive plantings of elms were forced into the tree removal business. There were plenty of dead elms up and down the streets where I delivered newspapers when I was a boy. One windy day I saw a massive branch from one such dead elm fall and take down the two-car garage beneath it. Admittedly, the garage might have been as old as the elm, but it collapsed as completely as a fallen house of cards.

Although young and vigorous elms line watercourses and dot open areas throughout the Northeast, most of the old city trees are long gone. I say most because, unlike the blight that completely decimated the chestnut population during the first decade of the twentieth century, Dutch elm disease was not universally deadly. There are still a few century-old trees around. Not many, to be sure, but enough to conclude that some either survived the infection or are resistant to it. The Cady Street elm fits into one of those categories and may be the oldest elm tree in town. It has certainly outlasted the farmhouse it once shaded—there is nothing left of it but a foundation.

Monet used contrast to capture the play of light and shadow beneath the Broadmore oak, and so too must I if the effect is going to be believable. The artist's term for the lightness or darkness of a color is "value," and as I mix some purple for the shadows I deepen the value by adding ultramarine. At this time of year it's easy to see only green; the color is everywhere, in myriad shades and variations. Intellectually, I know that green grass in shadow has not changed color. But artistic intent is often at odds with the intellect, and I mass-in the area beneath the elm with blued manganese violet. Getting the color right isn't necessary—it's contrast that will make this picture work, and the violet will provide a lively dark that I can work into as the painting develops. Handled correctly, it will carry as grass in shadow. Right now in this initial stage it looks like a grape-juice spill.

An artist can have a tough time in the middle of summer in the Northeast. The color green becomes so universal and pervasive that reportedly Georgia O'Keefe moved to the Southwest just to get away from it. The green canopy cuts off our view of the sky. Beneath our feet, green grass and weeds seem a continuous carpet. Every tree and shrub and weed is green, all because they are in the photosynthesis business.

No matter how commonplace, no matter how much we might take it for granted, there is a continuous miracle going on inside each leaf. The chlorophyll within the leaf makes the sugars and starches that are the foodstuff for everything that is alive on earth. Without it there would be no life, animal or otherwise. The process makes every harvest possible. Green is not only the color of summer, it is the color of life.

As a byproduct of photosynthesis, leaves cool and replenish the atmosphere around us. When sweltering city folk dream of the cool countryside, the image is not an imagined mirage—it actually is cooler and fresher in the country, or any other place where there are trees and plants to renew the air. Leaves trade carbon dioxide for oxygen, thus reversing the process of our own bodies and machines. They evaporate water, so much so that a mature tree will return a hundred and fifty gallons of water to the atmosphere on a warm summer day. Every green leaf takes part in the process. On an individual basis it might seem insignificant, but when multiplied by the billions of leaves around us on any given day in July, it can be dramatic in its impact.

Here on Cady Street this elm is still producing its own special kind of shade, even if the farmhouse it was planted to cool is nothing more than a crumbling foundation. The breeze stirs the leaves high overhead, and the small pools of sunlight blink and dance across the shaded grass.

The initial massing of the painting is completed. In honor of Georgia O'Keefe, I have refrained, thus far, from mixing greens, but they'll be part of the overlay in the next step. After an hour in front of the easel, it's time for a walk into the subject matter to enjoy the July midday in the shade of the Cady Street elm.

* * *

Young red-tailed hawks are learning to hunt during these first weeks of July, and not doing too good a job of it. They act like fast cars with bad brakes; they crash into power lines and bushes and, as I'm enjoying its shade, the Cady Street elm. Afterward, the young hawk sits on a nearby utility pole looking disheveled and dazed.

It all seems comical in a Marx Brothers sort of way, but it has to be a controlling factor on the hawk population. If a young hawk breaks a wing during the learning process—and it seems apparent that such damage is not an unusual event—it's the end of the line for that particular bird.

There was a time when I tried to become a hawk expert. By that, I mean I was going to become someone who could identify more hawks than the ubiquitous redtails and the little sparrow hawks on the roadside fence wires. I worked at my education for a few months one summer, and I always had binoculars and bird books at the ready. It soon became painfully evident that most species had light and dark morphs and completely different adult and juvenile plumages. The males of some species are different than females—in some instances, completely so. Size variants overlap. There are geographic variations, seasonal plumages, and infinite degrees of variety and differences. Then there's the fact that the names of hawks sound like adjectives but aren't; red-shouldered hawks don't have red shoulders, sharp-shinned hawks don't have sharp shins, and if you would identify a rough-legged hawk, don't look for rough legs. I finally gave up.

But I still enjoy watching hawks, even if I can't always tell one species from another. Among the few things I managed to learn is that the most visible of the hawks are the family known as buteos. You've seen them sailing high overhead in the summer—they seem to be able to glide forever without beating their wings. Red-tailed hawks outnumber all the other buteos put together, so if you have to guess what kind of large hawk you're looking at, a redtail is a safe bet. This bird's name is about as close as we come to a descriptive handle in the hawk family. Having said that, it should be noted that only the top side of the tail feathers are colored terra-cotta red, and immature birds have a nondescript gray brown tail.

Hawks spend most of their waking hours hunting. There is a fascination in trying to figure out what they're doing; northern harriers (marsh hawks) hover in the air, waiting for a hiding mouse to reappear; kestrels float and drift and reverse, every bit as maneuverable as the flying bugs they feed on; Cooper's hawks speed along through backyards and woodlands, hoping to surprise a squirrel or a songbird; red-tailed hawks soar like high altitude bombers, ready to become a falling bomb when their target appears. Hawks make their living while operating in full view of anyone who wants to observe them.

That's me, an observer. I'm not a devoted birder, and I may not always know exactly what I'm seeing, but I'm in love with the looking. And, in early July, it's fun to watch the antics of the young redtails earning their wings. They haven't quite mastered the maneuver at the end of a power dive, but they're getting closer with each mistake.

* * *

A man will tell you he has no interest in gardening. Yet, stored in his garage are several bags of fertilizers, insecticides and herbicides. There are irrigation devices and a half-dozen agricultural implements and at least one expensive motorized harvesting machine, yet he is not a farmer or a horticulturist.

No. Instead, he is the most common of suburbanites—a homeowner. His home, of course, has a lawn. Thus, he is no different from the rest of us. From April until October we all fight weeds and grubs and fungus that we can't even see. We fertilize and lime, we rake and thatch, we water and mow, and more than anything else, we worry. Having a lawn is a lot like owning an English sports car: as soon as a broken something is repaired, another thing fails—it's never in 100 percent running condition.

And for what? We don't enjoy our lawns as we should—the sign reads "Keep off the Grass" after all. Just how did we manage to get ourselves into the business of growing grass? Not many of us have grazing animals in the yard, and the Indians haven't attacked for a while, so the colonist's excuse that we need a clear field of fire won't hold much water. So why all the bother?

Pastures and meadows exist naturally in nature, but lawns are man's own creation. William Blake, the English poet, used the rose as a symbolic element of mankind's quest to master nature. Today, a far better choice would be the suburban lawn. That's something to ponder as we walk behind the mower on a sunny Saturday afternoon in July, when we're on a blind date with summer and the grass seems to grow as fast as we can cut it.

Sometimes it's tempting to wish for a meadow rather than a lawn, but one man's meadow is another man's weed patch. And in the Northeast, even meadows must be mown if they are not to become brushy fields within a year or two, which soon after grow to sumac and gray birch and then become second-growth forest, all in the space of fifteen or twenty years.

Weeds—all of them—demonstrate nature's constant and democratic need to clothe the earth. Other parts of the world have sand storms and suffer erosion of every kind. Weeds keep that from happening in the Northeast. Here and there you might find a gravel bank or a sandy spot where nothing seems to grow, but for the most part the land in New England covers itself, and weeds are responsible for keeping the ground clothed.

In their persistence, weeds are amazing in a discouraging sort of way. Farmers and gardeners hate them because they steal the space and nutrients intended for cultivated plants. When the word weed is used as a verb, it is synonymous with culling and removal. We show weeds a begrudging admiration in everyday vernacular when we say that something "grows like a weed." Some local weeds, such as gill (really a form of mint) and mustard (historically grown for its greens and only recently spread on hot dogs) long ago escaped from man's garden and have been persistently trying to get back in ever since.

Dandelions and thistle are famous for their parachute distribution, but most weed seeds have the consistency of ground pepper and are lightweight enough to be similarly blown around. On a breezy day, the water dish in the dog kennel collects a sample of weed seeds. They look like specs of dirt, but a close examination shows them for what they are. Some weed seed can be buried for forty years, yet when the soil is turned, it sprouts anew. It seems the smaller the seed, the hardier it is. And if there is any doubt about the number of weed seeds everywhere, watch a flock of juncos or chipping sparrows on a snowless day in winter. They're on the ground—sometimes on my concrete patio—using what must be microscopic vision to find weed seeds that humans cannot discern. They feed themselves all winter, each bird eating thousands of tiny seeds each day, yet still the weeds reappear every spring.

Weeds were never strangers to my lawn. Prospering out there was the standard assortment of crabgrass and creeping Charlie and a half-dozen other undesirables whose names I'd have to look up. But until a few years ago there was never any nut grass. That's the bright green, coarse stuff. In hot weather it grows so fast that two days after mowing it's sticking up again, making the lawn look worse than if you hadn't mowed in the first place.

There was never any of it in the lawn until an industrial park took over the field where I exercised the dogs and I had to find a new location. Nut grass, when uncut, grows tall and produces a burrlike seed that becomes entangled in the fur of animals, including dogs. The new place I found was full of it. Thus, as part of nature's plan, the botanical weed patch that I pass off as a lawn now has nut grass growing among the dandelions.

Chapter Six

HOT DAYS, WARM NIGHTS, AND A BRASSY SUN

August comes with hot days, warm nights, a
brassy sun, and something in the air that begins to
rust the high-hung leaves of the elms . . . August is
Summer thinking of the cut and color of her
Autumn costume.

–Hal Borland, *Twelve Moons of the Year*

There is often a pause between seasons, an apparent respite from the steady march of the year's progress. For a few weeks, it seems, everything is in balance, and nature appears to be in no hurry to move on to the next season.

There's one such interlude at the end of autumn when it seems the world is in recess, waiting for something that will set the clock in motion again. That "something," of course, is the first snowfall of winter. There is a similar pause once winter is over and spring hasn't yet begun. To someone eagerly anticipating all that spring has to offer, that particular lull can seem like a prison sentence. The pause goes on until the first series of warm days shakes nature out of its doldrums and gets springtime off and running.

Here at the end of summer we're in another of nature's pauses that can stretch for five or six weeks. For want of a better name, it's called *August.* Earlier in the season every rain brought a new spurt of growth immediately in its wake. It seemed then that all of nature was in a race to maturity, hastened by summer heat and long days of sunshine. But now, on the far side of summer's halfway point, things have slowed down and the urgency has disappeared.

There are no holidays on the calendar during the month of August. Perhaps that's because the entire month is a supposed to be a holiday. The August pause amounts to nature announcing that fall will be here soon enough. For now, the early work is over and it's time to sit back and enjoy the weather.

The tall mullen weeds at the roadside could be the poster child for this late-summer pause. From the steeplelike cluster of buds on their woody spike, mullens open just a few yellow flowers at a time—a couple today, another few tomorrow. By the end of summer the sequential blooms will have worked their way to the top of the bud tower, but right now the plant seems in no hurry to finish its work. It is August, after all.

Despite the apparent lull, the season continues its inexorable march toward autumn. There are signs, if one cares to notice them. The days are growing shorter and although the long summer twilight still lingers, it's dark by 8:30 on an August evening. The orioles have finished nesting and have departed for points south, leaving only their intricately woven nest high in the tallest red oak in the neighborhood. Down at the pond, May's fuzzy goslings are now indistinguishable from their parents as they waddle on the grass, each family still grouped and separated from their neighbors. The catalpa trees that blossomed so profusely in June now show long seed pods that hang like stalactites below the screening foliage. The petunias in the flower boxes have grown sparse and leggy, and some merciless pruning is in order if they are to rejuvenate and continue blooming through the autumn.

Clues, all of them, and one needn't be a detective to conclude that autumn is on its way. But it's easy to ignore the evidence—it's been short-sleeve weather for the past three months. On an August afternoon just off Main Street we turn a blind eye to the obvious and instead allow ourselves to believe that summer will go on forever. Oh, our intellectual side knows otherwise, but our emotional being takes off his shoes and goes for a walk on the new-cut grass.

* * *

Today I am out to paint a watercolor of the Fort River in the long light of morning. Earlier in the spring I was in the same water with rod and reel, but the trout are safe from me today. I'm working on a quarter-sheet sketch, just making notes rather than attempting a finished painting. Outdoors, the light changes much too rapidly for anything more than that.

Knowing he only had a sparse fifteen minutes of the "right light" to work with, John Singer Sargent posed the same two children in the gathering twilight every evening for an entire summer in order to finish his painting of the lighting of Chinese lanterns. That sort of persistence is not for me. My large paintings are nearly always done in the studio from a combination of sketches and photos made on location.

By the time I've finished a value sketch and penciled in the mass-outlines for the painting, swallows have gathered over the river. There must be a hatch of waterborne insects going on. The swallows swoop and glide just over the surface, feeding as they fly. There must be thirty of them. In flight they seem to dip and float in time to an unheard waltz. Their flight paths intercept and overlap each other's, yet there is never a collision. I put the painting aside and permit myself to be entertained.

Of the half-dozen kinds of swallows in the East, the only one that I can positively identify on the wing is the long-tailed barn swallow. But the birds I am looking at are streamlined little short-tailed swallows with a pale underside and a dark chinstrap, and, in truth, I'm unsure just what type they might be.

Sometimes bird identification takes detective work. The guide book says there are three species of swallows that nest in colonies and forage as flocks, just as these are doing. That narrows it down. Of the three, cliff swallows and purple martins are high-flying feeders, so by the process of elimination (and coupled with the clue of the chinstrap markings,) this flock must be bank swallows. You've seen them—or at least the series of holes they dig—in exposed sandy banks along roadsides or at gravel pits.

All swallows chatter a little as they fly but don't really have a song as such. Music is hardly necessary when you fly like something from a choreographer's imagination. Now a few barn swallows have mixed in with the feeding flock, and if the others are flying in waltz time, the barn swallows are absolute poetry in flight. They seem to fly effortlessly, and flash their long swallowtails as they loop the ends of their turns. An articulate person might describe them as elegant.

Swallows are famous for eating mosquitoes, and people will go to great lengths to encourage these birds to nest in their yard. Long before the Europeans came along, Indians hollowed out gourds and placed them on tall poles around their villages to attract purple martins. They did it for all the same reasons folks put up those multiple-dwelling affairs in their backyards today. If a swallow colony decides to move into one of those apartment-block bird-houses, they're usually back year after year.

But people who assume swallows are the answer to their bug problems are forgetting about the balance of nature: if the birds are to remain in the area, there has to be an abundance of food. That means mosquitoes in a quantity that is more than the birds can eat. If the swallows ate all the bugs (as the human residents hope they will) they would have nothing to eat tomorrow and would leave to look for food elsewhere. There has to be a balance. For the birds to stay in the area there has to be enough food for them to eat on a continuous basis. Unfortunately for the human residents, that excess translates to a guarantee they'll keep scratching mosquito bites.

When I return to the painting, I indicate the yellow sunlit fields beyond the shadowy woods with washes of aureolin. August is far and away the yellowiest month of the year—the entire world seems to turn that loveliest of colors. There are the familiar black-eyed Susans and daisy-like wild sunflowers that have been blooming since July. There is hawkweed in waste places, looking like small dandelions on two-foot stems. Even the leaves and grasses lose their early summer vibrancy and fade to sere shades of ochre and amber at this time of year.

But, more than anything else, what colors August is goldenrod. Like all wildflowers, nobody pays it much attention before it blossoms. But then late summer arrives and every vista is colored bright mustard yellow. It's hard to imagine how much goldenrod there is in the world until it comes to flower in August. For years it was thought to be a cause of hay fever, but we've recently understood that the blame lies elsewhere. In one form or another, it grows just about everywhere—there is a woodland variety, and I've seen another type growing in the sand dunes of Cape Cod. If goldenrod serves no other purpose than to color the month of August, it does its job well.

* * *

On the drive home from my painting session, I stop by Ron's house. Or, more accurately, I stop by Ron's garden. Since the first blush of spring fever drove the gardener out to his plot, he has fought weeds and bugs, watered and fertilized, and nearly broken his back from bending over. The spring garden produced abundantly, but there are times when even the most enthusiastic of gardeners wonders if it's all worthwhile because right around the time the backyard Kentucky Wonder green beans come in, they're available for thirty-nine cents a pound at the local farm stand.

But then August arrives, and the first of the beefsteak tomatoes are on the table and the ears of sweet corn are shucked, and any doubts the gardener might have had regarding his efforts vanish in the steam swirling over the kettle where the corn is starting to boil. Tomatoes and sweet corn—the two are forever linked in the minds of those whose mouths water at the mention of the word August. We gladly trade the heat and humidity of midsummer for steaming ears of butter-and-sugar corn and sliced sun-ripened beefsteaks. With just a sprinkle of salt, if you please.

Oh, there's been sweet corn for sale at the supermarket for the past month or so, but those ears were picked sometime last week in a field five hundred miles to the south. After five or six days, they no more resemble fresh sweet corn than a dill pickle resembles a fresh cucumber. Lovers of sweet corn know that the time from field to pot should be kept to a minimum, so much so that it seems the water ought to be boiling before the trip to the garden. In August, roadside farm stands pop up everywhere, often with just a single word on their signs—CORN. Those that succeed know their continued business hinges on the veracity of the unspoken word "fresh."

When the tomatoes come in, the wait is finally over. The tasteless hothouse-grown pretenders offered year 'round at the supermarket are quickly forgotten. In July there might be cherry tomatoes and short-season early varieties, but those are just a preview of August's main-season giants. Earlier, the discussion had run to whether Better Boy was superior to Jet Star, or if the old standby Beefsteak might not be supplanted by one of the new hybrids. Ron favors a variety named Early Girl, and who can argue with him? His explanation is that it is an early tomato with midseason heft and flavor, and since the vines are indeterminate, they continue to grow and produce right up until the frost. Ron estimates that he gets a hundred tomatoes off each vine during the course of a summer.

When I depart after my visit, I'm loaded down with what would be a week's worth of tomatoes for a family of eight. I feel like a character from the children's story about the Little Red Hen; Ron has done all the work in the garden, and I show up in time to take home the gratuitous bounty.

I used to say that someone could make a fortune if he could just figure out a way to offer August's sweet corn and tomatoes in February. At that time of year, when winter has overstayed its welcome, people would pay a great deal for the taste of a real summer tomato or fresh corn on the cob.

At least I would.

But now we have "fresh frozen" corn-on-the-cob available throughout the year, and "cluster tomatoes on the vine," which are a far cry from run-of-the-mill flavorless hothouse tomatoes. Although they're not the same as the late-summer corn and tomatoes that come from Ron's garden, they're pretty close.

Unfortunately, neither sells very well. But perhaps it's a matter of some things being so closely tied to a particular season that sweet corn-on-the-cob and sun-ripened juicy tomatoes just insult the senses at any time other than late summer.

But when it's here, for just a short time we are permitted to taste a little bit of heaven.

* * *

Ron and I walk out to inspect his orchard. He grows several varieties of apples, and all are plumping up here at the tail end of summer. They'll be ready for harvest in another month.

The farmer tends his orchard all through the year, pruning and shaping and spraying and fertilizing his trees, all to influence the quality and quantity of the apple harvest. The trees themselves need no such attention. As if to prove it, they grow wild all throughout the Northeast.

Sometimes wild-growing trees produce apples that look like

those for sale at a farm stand, but mostly not. Wild apples are usually small and if not bug-eaten, at least bug-sampled. During the fall I often bring home Greenings and Cortlands and Russets from the abandoned orchards where I hunt grouse, but they always go into pies, never the fruit bowl.

Today, with fruit from every corner of the world available year 'round at the corner market, it is almost impossible to imagine the importance of the apple in the American pantry one hundred years ago. The keeping quality of apples made them the only fresh fruit available for most of the year. Every farm had a fruit cellar for storage. In those hardscrabble times, apples were often the only sweet in a farm family's diet, and they were made into preserves of every imaginable kind.

Cider has become something of an autumn curiosity, but it, too, was an indispensable part of the countryman's diet. Before the advent of refrigeration, cider was often the only alternative to water, and Americans had it on the table at mealtime in much the same way that Europeans drink wine with their meals.

Antique shops are filled with unusual wooden utensils that seem to have no modern-day equivalent. There are short shovels and scoops and paddles and rakes and a long-handled curiosity labeled a "cheese cutter," all made entirely of an unfamiliar, pale wood with a decidedly twisted grain. All of them were used in processing apple products. The old traditions were that anything used to process cider or apple preserves had to be made from apple wood.

Jonathan Chapman didn't have to become Johnny Appleseed to fill the landscape with apple trees—the American farmer did it for him. Apples were the staff of life for the countryman of less than a century ago, and orchards were a necessary part of every homestead.

* * *

I have the truck's windows rolled down as I drive home through the oppressive heat of the afternoon. The leaves on the trees along the roadside begin to roll over in the wind and show their silvery undersides. When I was a kid, my grandmother would say, "Look, it's getting ready to rain. See how the leaves are turning over?"

And she would always be right. Within minutes, the sky would darken and there would be a downpour.

On August afternoons like this, I remember Mémère and her bit of weather wisdom. It's been hot all day, and earlier the sky was full of puffy cumulus clouds. Then later in the afternoon, as a predictable function of the heat, thunderheads started to rear-up over the distant hills. Far away they looked like distant mountain ranges above the summer haze. When they came closer, they appeared as plum-colored areas that darkened the skyline. The chilled air that accompanies the thunderstorm circulates as wind, often in a direction contrary to the prevailing breeze of summer, and thus flips tree leaves onto their backs.

Sometimes when a man is busy with his outdoor work, he doesn't notice the approaching storm until suddenly there's a gust of cool air—sometimes it's twenty degrees cooler. An instantaneous drop from eighty-five degrees to sixty-five can be as shocking as stepping into a walk-in freezer.

Usually, though, the distant rumble of thunder is felt as much as heard, and the gardener straightens up from his work in the flower bed and looks at the approaching weather. He might hurry around and roll up the car windows and drag the lawn chairs under cover so they won't blow away.

Then, if he's still the little boy that I used to be, he will sit on the front steps under the overhang and watch the lightning show as the thunderstorm rolls through. Sometimes there are hailstones —the ice is a nonsequitur in the heat of August and a potential disaster for farmers with crops still in the field—but usually it's only wind-whipped rain in big, shirt-soaking drops. Afterward, the rain gauge reveals how much precipitation fell. It's always a surprise. The earth in mid-August is usually thirsty, and a rainfall that at another time of the year would have threatened to overflow the storm drains is often soaked up like a sponge.

Once the storm has passed, the yard is littered with wind-blown leaves and detritus driven out of the trees. The oaks lining my backyard always seem to lose a few leafy twigs. There might be a rainbow if the storm passes directly to the east, but usually by the time I locate the camera it has pretty well faded away.

But the thundershower always acts like some atmospheric catharsis, and for a little while the air is washed clean and the sky is clarified. Once the sun rewarms the wet grass, the humidity will rise again, but for that brief, cool half-hour after the storm it seems the heat wave is over and we can permit ourselves to believe that autumn is just around the corner.

* * *

Tonight something occurs that only comes once in a blue moon: We actually have a blue moon. The full moon rising out of the eastern tree line looks normal enough—it's as bright and yellow as a newly minted gold medallion—but it's a blue moon nonetheless.

We don't pay much attention to the moon's phases these days. For a suburbanite it's just a curiosity, really, and many calendars no longer carry the symbols for the moon's phases in the square below the date. But not so many years ago the illumination of the moon was hugely important to people who lived off the land.

For a farmer trying to get a crop out of the field, a few evenings of moonlight could make all the difference in the world. The full moon rose with the setting sun and provided moonlight all night long. The almost-full phases in the days before and just after the actual full-moon date were almost as bright, but the rising and setting times advanced about an hour per day and didn't produce an entire night's worth of moonlight.

People traveled by night and built barns and houses with the lunar calendar in mind to ensure they'd have enough light to work by. And in the reverse of that logic, there were other more secretive things that were best done by the dark of the moon.

The Indians measured the passing of time by the moon's phases. Any kid who ever watched the Lone Ranger remembers Tonto speaking in terms of "many moons since we ride this trail, Kimosabe."

In a perfect world—at least, a perfect world for calendar makers —each month would start with a new moon. But a complete lunar cycle measures slightly more than twenty-nine and a half days, so like everything else celestial, it doesn't quite jibe with any time-keeping system that would be convenient for us living down here on the blue planet. The Indians, who didn't mind if things didn't line up in an orderly fashion, accepted the imperfection and had a name for each month based on the cycle of the moon's phases. Their months were named Wolf Moon, Beaver Moon, Snow Moon, and so on. It didn't always work out to the sort of thing you could set your watch by today, and sometimes they had to insert an extra moon into the year to make things agree with the solstice and equi-nox. But they managed.

The European settlers adopted some of the Indians' names for the moons as they appeared on their calendar. July's was Buck Moon, and that was followed by August's Sturgeon Moon. The colonists chose their own name for September's and called it Harvest Moon. Ah, but once in a while, as is the case here in August, the full moon occurs on the first or second day of the month. Twenty-nine and one-half days later, there's another full moon, but the calendar page hasn't been flipped over yet. What are we going to call this nameless second full moon of the month?

For reasons I don't understand, it became a blue moon. The word blue may have had another meaning centuries ago, but it's lost to modern times, and we're left with blue laws, bluenoses, blue movies, and a blue moon.

In some years, if the sequence is just right, there will be two blue moons on the calendar, but then several years will pass before we see another. If the numbers line up it can happen in any month of the year except February. But it's uncommon—something that happens once in a . . . Well, at least we know where that expression comes from.

Now, when it's not quite September just off Main Street, it's pleasant to get away from the streetlamps and take a walk in the moonlight. As bright as it seems across the park, the eyes strain to discern colors without much success. June's fireflies are just an evening memory. The crickets chirp and the katydids scrape, and it's enough to know that the abundance of August not only brings us hot days, warm nights and a brassy sun, but sometimes a second full moon.

Chapter Seven

THE PROMISE OF ANOTHER AUTUMN

September is the year at the turn . . . time
hastening and days shortening . . . the wonder
and fulfillment and the ever-amazing promise
of another autumn.

–Hal Borland, *Sundial of the Seasons*

In the time of Imperial Rome, Julius Caesar changed the old Roman calendar around and started the year in January rather than March. At the same time, he changed the name of the first month of summer to July, after himself. Not to be outdone, his successor, Caesar Augustus, renamed the second summer month August. Even from this distance it all seems a bit vain. But, then again, they were emperors.

September had been the seventh month of the year under the pre-Caesar system. The "Sept" part of that name refers to seven in Latin. Similarly, the "Oct" in October's name indicates that it was the eighth month, the "Nov" in November is nine, and the "Dec" in December is ten. But when they were realigning the calendar, the

Romans didn't think to change the names of the numbered months leftover from the previous system. It seems bizarre that after 2000 years nobody has bothered to fix that obvious non sequitur. Evidently, they ran out of good names.

Society's verbal bad habits have gone far beyond the calendar. In nature, all known things have been formally named, but then we insist on giving nicknames to everything. To make matters worse, we can't seem to agree what those nicknames should be. It results in vernacular confusion, and, unlike the calendar, we can't blame it on the ancient Romans.

I was once in Kansas, warming my hands by a woodstove in the barn of a local rancher/friend. We had been following my dogs around his pastures on my annual winter quail-hunting trip. The fire crackled, and after an afternoon outdoors in the cold, the heat was more than welcome. When I asked what my Kansas friend burned for firewood, I got a fast lesson in local lingo.

"We burn oak and thorn and some hedge, but the best stuff is red elm," he told me.

The city boy from back East must have looked puzzled. I was okay with oak. Kansas has an easily identified variety called burr oak, named for its hairy acorn caps. It's a part of the white oak family, and if it's at all like the white oak we're familiar with in the East, it makes wonderful firewood. But what was "thorn?" And "hedge?" And I had never heard of "red" elm.

It took some cross-examination, but I found out that thorn is the local name for honey locust. In Kansas, locust grows so thorny that even squirrels won't climb it. It has thorns growing out of other thorns in nasty, nestlike clumps. But it is desirable wood that produces an intensely hot fire.

Hedge, it turns out, is the species that everybody west of the Mississippi calls Osage orange. If you listen closely you'll hear them call it "damn hedge," even if they don't actually say damn. It is an invasive tree in pastures and along streambeds, and ranchers spend a lot of time trying to get rid of it. The wood burns a lot like hemlock, with a snap-crackle-and-pop shower of sparks.

And red elm is the local Kansas name for slippery elm. It is dense and straight-grained and makes wonderful firewood; it's not at all like the American elm we know here in the East.

Honey locust, Osage orange, slippery elm—those are the proper names, but nobody in Kansas uses them. I've spent time totaling nearly a year in the state but have never heard anyone use terms other than thorn, hedge, and red elm for those trees.

Everything in nature seems to have several names. As if the conflict between local vernacular and official names weren't enough, sometimes nicknames change with the season as the appearance of the plant or animal changes. Wild clematis is called virgin's bower in the springtime, and it later becomes old man's beard when the leaves have fallen and the blossoms have shriveled to lacy filaments. Queen Anne's lace becomes birds' nest weed as soon as it's done flowering. The weasel becomes an ermine and the hare becomes a snowshoe rabbit when their coats change color to winter white.

The scientific name is sometimes the only way to pin down what it is we're talking about. There are two unrelated trees in the northeast woods correctly called hornbeam. The appearance of the smooth bark on the American hornbeam *(Carpinus caroliniana)* has been compared to the muscles in a strong man's arm. It in no way resembles the scaly bark of the hop hornbeam *(Ostrya virginiana.)* To make matters worse, both trees are also nicknamed ironwood.

Dolphin is the proper name of both a fish (the mahimahi) and a marine mammal (the porpoise) Each creature swims in salt water, but other than that they are related to one another about as closely as I am to my pet canary.

People have moles in their lawn and buy gopher bait to get rid of them. Gopher bait is usually strychnine-treated corn that will kill neighborhood squirrels and chipmunks, but not lawn moles.

Those moles eat worms and insect grubs and will crawl right past the poisoned corn that lawn owners put out for them. Pocket gophers, for whom the bait is designed, are ratlike rodents that do not geographically occur anywhere near the Northeast. The only thing moles and gophers have in common is they both make underground tunnels. Nevertheless, our garden supply stores stock and sell a lot of gopher bait. To confuse things even further, in some parts of the South a gopher is a tortoise, and he won't eat strychnine-laced corn, either.

If people can't tell a mole from a gopher, consider that we live in a world where Jack Russell is a dog, Dolly Varden is a trout, Bob White is a game bird, and Joe Pye is a weed. We sometimes name things for what they look like rather than what they really are, and end up with a sweet potato that is not a potato, a robin that is really a thrush, and a pronghorn antelope that's actually a type of goat. Of course, foot-long hot dogs aren't, and a two-by-four is neither two nor four, so maybe it really doesn't matter.

The verbal disorder continues and shows no signs of ever clarifying itself. Even if the word September no longer has its original meaning, all the images that word conjures up are no less valid. The ninth month by any other name would be just as wonderful.

* * *

Earlier, there was mist at sunrise—not the sort of murky haze that is generated by the high humidity in the dog days of July, but a clean breath of autumn in the air. Now, at 8 A.M., the sun has chased the mist from the hollows and a clear September day is in store, and the breeze ruffles the first of the autumn leaves in the treetops.

I'm in the woods this morning searching for mushrooms. When the summer ferns begin to die, they produce a not-unpleasant smell that I associate with fall. The air is heavy with an aroma that is every bit as evocative of autumn as the fragrance of hay is of

June. The showery late-summer weather over the past two weeks has awakened the woodland mushrooms, and they now appear nearly everywhere, pushing their way up through the leaf litter literally overnight. They're unlike anything else that grows in the woods, and I find them fascinating.

Mushrooms survive above ground for weeks, but there is a "right" day to pick them. It's easy to be too late, since the mushroom picker is in a race with the bugs. Inspection is a matter of breaking the cap. If the flesh is clean, the mushroom goes into the collection basket. If bugs have gotten a start on the interior, I let them finish their meal and leave the mushroom on the forest floor.

When I was a kid I didn't like to eat mushrooms. They were just something to be scraped off a steak, so I never bothered to learn much about them. The few I pick now are passed along to my father-in-law. He dries them for later use in soups and in a particular ersatz puff pastry that is too wonderful for ordinary tastes.

There are only a few varieties whose edibility I'm certain of; I look for spongy-bottomed bolite mushrooms that the Polish call "prawdziwy" *(prav-GEE-vê.)* There are many bolite varieties, but the three I seek out are the heavy-stemmed king bolites; redtops, which are properly named scaberstalks; and the easily identified goldstalk. I won't take a chance on anything that changes color when broken, and none of those three will. I also pick giant puffballs and hen-of-the-woods when I stumble across them, but after that I leave everything else in the mushroom world alone.

Other mushroom pickers tell me that oyster mushrooms are easy to spot and that the variety called morels are worth seeking out. Meadow mushrooms are common and supposedly very good to eat. I'm pretty sure I can differentiate chanterelles from the similar, but poisonous, jack-o-lantern mushrooms, but I'm not going to bet on it.

Sometimes I think I should try to learn more about the edible kinds of mushrooms. I'm an outdoorsman, after all, and I should know these things. Just about everything I've ever learned has come from books, and there are plenty of books on mushrooms.

But then I consider this salient fact: I own a collection of field guides on birds and trees and wildflowers. In spite of my library, I can't tell one female warbler from another. The various kinds of ash trees remain a mystery to me, even with the book in my hand. And I forget the names of most wildflowers as soon as I look them up. And here's the important part—I'm not eating any of them.

Every field guide to mushrooms opens with a disclaimer that amounts to, *Don't believe anything you read in this book!* If nothing else, I believe the disclaimer. I'll stick with the September king bolites that I'm sure of, and during the rest of the year I'll pick up my fresh mushrooms at the supermarket.

* * *

Susan asked me how I had bruised my shin. I told her I had hit it on the oven door. Since the wall oven in our kitchen is mounted at eye level, my answer didn't make much sense until I told her the door I had smacked was attached to an old stove that had been thrown out in the Tripwire covert, where I had been exercising the dogs the day before. In the tall weeds, I hadn't noticed that the oven door was open.

People used to throw their discarded stuff out into the street, but one of the functions of civilization is to protect the public from its own bad habits, so we created public dumps. But times change. Now, when people bring something like an unwanted kitchen stove to the dump, they are charged a disposal fee. Is it any wonder that it ends up by the side of a dirt road in the Tripwire covert? Oh, responsible people take care of their junk properly, and will pay fees when necessary. But if society was made up of only responsible people, we wouldn't need keys and locks and safety-seal packaging, and banks wouldn't put leashes on their ballpoint pens.

I recently had an opportunity to fill out a personality profile for an outfit that was selling my books. One of the questions was, "What is sure to get you to your boiling point?"

My one word answer was (and still is) "litter." Trash thrown out carelessly and thoughtlessly—or, even worse, on purpose—is a lasting curse on the environment. There are plenty of things wrong with the world, but litter is one that we do to ourselves. It is 100 percent preventable.

A symptom of society's disconnect from nature is the habit of tossing paper cups and hamburger wrappers out the car window. The guy who dumped the stove in the Tripwire covert is guilty of a lot more than thoughtlessness, but what about casual litterers and their cups and wrappers? They are living in their own little world, of course. Since they didn't want those items any longer, they threw them away. For them, "away" is any place not in their world.

Too bad. That sort of mindlessness implies that as individuals we don't matter in the overall scheme of things. We regularly hear that the earth belongs to all of us, with all the responsibility and obligation implied in that verb. But I wonder. Are those mindless litterers and dumpers right? Are we really just passengers on the earth? Am I wrong to think that you and I are actually a part of it all?

When I went to sea, we who worked on the ship were considered "part of the venture." It was written into maritime law; as crew members, we had a legally bound obligation to the vessel and to the success of the voyage. We were a functioning and responsible part of the ship, and were obligated to its safety and success. Here on planet earth, are we part of the venture? Or are we "just playing pinochle in the bilge?" as Annie Dillard speculates in her insightful book, *Pilgrim at Tinker Creek.*

We have created a society in which most things are so worthless that after we buy them, we're expected to throw them out. The hard truth of that comes home to me every Friday when I carry the trash cans to the end of the driveway for pickup. Sometimes I look at what I've piled up and consider that I bought everything that is in those cans. It's all junk, of course, most of it packaging and of no use to anyone. But I spent money for all of it nonetheless.

At Bobby Sazama's farm in Hampden, Massachusetts, there is a little valley (called a "dingle" in local lingo) out behind the barn. It was the household's dump up until the town instituted trash pick up, which Bobby estimates was about 1960. His family has lived in the same place on North Road since the Civil War, and for a century that crease was the repository of everything that broke and was beyond repair. Most of the ditch is overgrown now, but I can still see some broken canning jars and pieces of dinner plates. I can also identify what used to be a wheel harrow. What amazes me most is that there really isn't much there—five generations' worth of trash from a working farm didn't amount to very much.

My own grandfather, as far as I know, didn't own much. Oh, he was a farmer, and as such he had farm tools and implements—harnesses for his horses and cultivators and the like. But as far as personal possessions, he had a nativity set that he put out at Christmas, and he owned and played a concertina. He had a good suit of clothes that he wore to church on Sundays and to his children's weddings. It seems to be the same suit in every photograph that I've ever seen of him, and apparently it lasted his whole life and he was buried in it. But that's it: a suit of clothes, a concertina, and a nativity set. He had little else in the way of personal effects, not even a pocket watch.

Then, I look around at the possessions that his grandson owns—most of it falling under the classification of toys—and I'm embarrassed. My house is full, and still I don't have enough room for my stuff.

At one time, a man might go through life and own just three or four pairs of shoes, not all at once, but during his lifetime. Things that wore out were repaired, including shoes. Old homes didn't have closets because people didn't have extra clothes to hang up. Things were made out of metal and wood, and any handyman could repair broken metal or make a replacement for a wooden part. There wasn't much to throw out. The dingle behind Bobby Sazama's barn is not unique—old time junk piles were small with good reason.

I recently took a personal excursion into the past when, out of necessity, I made a handle for a shovel. I say it was out of necessity, not because I had a pressing need for the shovel but because a replacement handle at the hardware store was priced several dollars more than a new shovel. That by itself is a comment on the convoluted economics of the times we live in. Cost-effective realities aside, I wasn't about to throw out the shovel's perfectly good business end for want of a new handle. So I went into the woods to find a replacement.

The clear-cut land along the brook behind my house initially resprouted to blackberry and viburnum, then ash saplings sprang up in their shade. There are thousands of potential shovel handles growing back there. I put my hand around one after another, trying to imagine it in its future role. I found a sapling with a bend in the right place. It was thick enough to take the shaping I needed to give it, and it didn't have any branches in the five-foot run of the trunk that I was going to use. And the price was right. More on my home-made handle further on.

We visit places like Old Sturbridge Village in central Massachusetts where people in period costumes go through the motions of representing life as it was lived when our nation was new. We see women spin wool into yarn and craftsmen make brooms or nails or wooden tool handles, and it becomes a form of entertainment. We're so far removed from what they're doing that it's difficult to connect the past the reenactors portray to our present way of life.

Yet, that's the real lesson of Sturbridge—not the quaintness of shaping wood, but the reality that just a few generations ago people made virtually everything they used, and that included a good deal more than shovel handles. Those self-sufficient Americans knew volumes about wood and leather and how to make tools at a forge. They knew about weaving cloth and grinding grain and canning the harvest from orchard and garden.

The industrial revolution, not that remote in our historical past, distanced the average person from nature in a way that six thousand years of previous civilization never did. Mass production has removed the necessity of developing the skills to make tools and the handiness to use them.

Some old tools have modern-day equivalents, and we can see how hammers and shovels and brooms have changed over the generations, and how they've remained the same, too. With others, since both the final product and the use for which that product was intended have disappeared, people can no longer imagine what the tool might have been used for. Our great-grandparents made barrels and buckets and baskets and wheels with wooden spokes, and they left behind a myriad of job-specific tools that have no job left to do.

In my favorite take on that phenomenon, I saw a hawker on television wondering out loud what anyone ever did with a cast-iron duck decoy. It didn't float, he astutely observed, so "it must have been a doorstop."

When it was legal to hunt ducks commercially, there was a type of floating duck blind called a sink box, essentially a raft with a below-water-level box in the middle. The hunter would get into the box, and weights would be placed on the raft to sink it to the level of the water's surface. Once that happened, the box would disappear below the surface of the water, and so would the hunter inside. Such a rig was anchored in a likely location and surrounded with decoys.

The weights that hunters used to weigh down the sink-box raft were made of cast iron and often shaped like ducks so they could do double-duty as decoys. These days, it's illegal to hunt out of sink boxes, so it baffles the imagination to find a use for a cast-iron decoy. But without some knowledge of the past, you might believe the ten-pound cast-iron duck had really been a doorstop.

If there are no automobiles one hundred years from now, won't people wonder what a radar detector was used for? Or what in the world those ubiquitous plastic ice scrapers are? Or snow chains?

But it's not just the tools that are antiques. There is an entire lost world of knowledge that it took mankind six thousand years to accumulate. The knowledge is about self-sufficiency. Today, how many of us could put up a supply of preserves as our grandparents did? Hitching up a team of horses is something of a specialty skill. Who knows how to drop a tree without killing himself? Or make a container that will hold water? Or even something as simple as darning a holed sock—who can do that any more?

After I cut the ash tree that was to be the shovel's new handle, there was fitting and adjusting to be done back in my workshop. I have a drawknife and a spokeshave that I use for decoy carving, and put them to good use on the ash sapling. The end that mates with the steel shovel had to be tapered and split, and the shaft was rounded to fit my hands comfortably. I smoothed it and rubbed a little linseed oil into the grain, then tapped the handle into place and fastened it with a single rivet.

I'm not skilled at handle making. The results weren't pretty. An old-time farmer would have had a supply of seasoned ash on hand rather than having to work with a freshly cut sapling. But the shovel was broken, and I did what I could. I gained an insight that simply inserting a manufactured, store-bought replacement never could have provided. Part of that revelation is bound up in the idea that people once did this sort of thing as a matter of daily living.

There is a wonderful satisfaction that comes of making something you need, yet "homemade" has become a disparaging adjective. Early Americans were so proud of the things they created that they invariably carved their names into them and usually included the date as well. They were aware of the times in which they lived and aware, too, that the implement they had made would probably out-live its maker. To me, that practice seemed a quaint sort of thing to do. But then I realized that I brand my name into every decoy I carve, and sign and date all my paintings. You'll have to look hard to find it, but I have my name on my homemade ash shovel handle, too.

Chapter Eight

A BRISK WIND IN THE TREETOPS

October is a brisk wind in the treetops, a whisper
among the crisp leaves, a breath of apple cider, a
gleam from a jack-o'-lantern, and the echo of
laughter under a full moon

–Hal Borland, *Sundial of the Seasons*

Sugar maples in the sunlight are what people from around the world come to New England to see in October. The almost incandescent color of the maples runs the spectrum from the purest bright amber and old gold to peach pink and a brilliant orange. There are supporting players in the high drama that is autumn: birches and aspens become masses of chartreuse, ashes run to a ruddy purple, sumac and swamp maples are brilliant crimson, and beech trees become the exact color of the yellow crayon in a kid's coloring book set. Dressed in their autumn foliage, the trees seem like an elaborate three-dimensional pointillist painting, with dabs of unexpected color shot here and there against a dark background provided by the pines and hemlocks.

Autumn in the Northeast is one of the very few things in nature that, upon first encounter by an outsider, is not vaguely disappointing. The colors are no less remarkable whether you are examining a single leaf in your hand or a hillside clothed in billions of them. For a short time in October, with the trees glowing clouds of foliage and the ground a carpet of amber and tan, the reflected sunlight is saturated with golden hues, and shadows are made of warm tones unseen at any other time of year. The very light itself is glowing with the colors of autumn.

Since words can't describe the stunning and ever-changing October spectacle, people in New England refer to it simply as *The Color*. And, in that respect, The Color is a bit puny this year. Oh, it's still magnificent, but for those of us who have seen more than a half-century of New England autumns, it is a fact that some are significantly better than others. This year, the leaves have colored less than brilliantly and are quickly falling off the trees. The swamp maple in my backyard, which usually turns the color of pinot noir, is a sickly yellow.

If the quality of the autumn spectacle can be predicted, it will take a better man than I to do it. Some years, when there's been plenty of rain and it seems the trees are brimming with life and ready to put on a spectacular autumn show, the leaves fall off as quickly as they turn color. In dry years when the trees are under stress, sometimes the leaves simply shrivel and fade, but in other apparently identically dry seasons we experience the most spectacular autumn of the decade. There must be a method of interpreting the factors, but I haven't yet figured it out. Instead, I'll just enjoy what the autumn brings. That part is easy.

* * *

October is bird-hunting season in the Northeast. I'm out today with the puppy, hunting for grouse—although to say a man with a bird dog is "hunting" is a bit of a stretch. Right now I'm following

Nancy, who is the one doing the actual hunting. She covers the ground at a steady run and searches out the likely places. When she finds a game bird, she performs that little magic trick that is a bird dog on point. I walk along behind her and take it all in, far more spectator than participant.

A dog trainer will tell you that every bird dog consists of two basic components: the all-important nose, and the rest of the dog. One definition says that second part is the life-support system for the nose. As trainers, we can address only that second part, the dog itself. I've taught Nancy to behave and to respond to commands and a few other small refinements. The really important stuff—the things that will make her a bird dog—are the things she does with her nose, and those are exclusively things she teaches herself. All I can do in that area is provide Nancy ample opportunity to give herself that education.

I've read opinions that a dog has a sense of smell a thousand times more powerful than man's. But I don't believe it. I've been watching dogs find birds for most of a lifetime, and it seems to me that they're not smelling when they hunt but, rather, scenting. The two are distinct and separate functions, as different as whistling is from singing, and the fact that both happen inside the nose only clouds the distinction between the two.

Animals, particularly mammals, live in a world where scent rather than sight is their primary means of gathering information. Homo sapiens seems to be alone in the animal kingdom in not having a scenting ability. (I'd be interested to find out if our close relatives in the primate family have the highly developed scenting ability of other animals.) In the evolutionary scheme of things, the loss of our ability to detect scent may have been part of the trade-off that saw us exchange claws and speed for nimble fingers and reasoning ability.

I could be wrong. It is possible that animal scent is like ultraviolet light and high-pitched sound, representing an end of the olfactory scale that we humans are unequipped to detect. Whatever the explanation. people cannot perceive scent in the same way that most animals can.

Yet men have been investigating the undetectable phenomenon for hundreds of years. The research has all been empirical in nature, and the instruments used have historically been the noses of hunting dogs rather than tools of the laboratory.

From those pragmatic observations, we can conclude that scent can be carried on the breeze, sometimes for great distances. We also know that humidity in the air improves scenting conditions, and very cold weather makes it all but impossible for a dog to scent much of anything. (Whether the scent itself doesn't disperse or the dog's nose stops working when the temperature is in the teens is something I can't answer.)

Scent seems to come in two varieties. *Foot scent* is laid down by an animal as it walks. There is evidently a directional quality to foot scent, since a hunting dog will immediately follow it in the right direction. Then there is *body scent,* which accumulates and puddles in still air and can be carried on the breeze or dispersed in a wind. The two are different because a pointing dog will follow foot scent but stop and point when it detects body scent.

Nancy demonstrates: from a full run she abruptly reverses direction and, with her head in the air, strikes out upwind. Her nose is elevated as she samples the messages on the breeze. At one point she momentarily looses the thread of scent and has to double back. Finally, she advances on a little clump of juniper and halts suddenly in midstride, her head straining toward the evergreen. She is locked in her pose, and her only motion is a trembling of her tail. Only a blind man couldn't read her message: "The bird is right here, Steve."

I have written that a bird dog on point is a magician performing a trick. This isn't the sort of charlatan magician who will fool you with slight-of-hand. That sort of thing is entertaining but never believable. In Nancy's case, the magic is real. She has found a grouse that was trying hard not be discovered, and I don't know how she did it.

Oh, I've got the basics down: "The dog scents the bird but arrests its instinct to pounce. The dog's point is the result of immobility caused by the tension of the opposing forces."

I know that.

But to point a running grouse the dog must approach the bird fast enough so that it realizes it can no longer outrun the dog, yet, at the same time, the dog must be cautious to prevent the bird from panicking and taking flight. Boldness and caution are diametrically opposed, but both are required if the magic is to happen. No dog trainer can teach that, but somehow a dog teaches itself.

The dog doesn't see the bird. The whole finding and trailing and pointing process is based on information somehow contained in scent. I don't know how dogs do it. Any explanation I might offer only leads to more questions without sound answers. It is humbling.

Maybe it's just as well. There is a danger in studying anything too closely, and that danger is letting the magic drain out. Nancy knows the answer to some of the questions I'm pondering, but on this October afternoon she's content to let me do the wondering.

* * *

In October, homeowners invariably become reacquainted with mice. They are everywhere—unless you're reading this on an airplane in flight, you're probably within fifty feet of a mouse. They populate every woodpile and will nest in anything that isn't moving. They move into my birdhouses as soon as the birds move out.

Mice have never received what could be called good press. Otherwise calm women scream in terror at their appearance. Farmers and storekeepers hate them. They are lumped in with lice, cockroaches, and rats under the label vermin (an evil-sounding word if ever there was one) and folks feel obliged to exterminate them. Society tends to judge animals by their worth to mankind, and mice rate a flat zero. There is, after all, no market for mouse pelts. There is no demand for rack-of-mouse in epicurean restaurants. If you scratch hard enough, someone might mention that mice eat weed seeds, but other than that no one has a kind word for them.

What would writers of children's fiction and cartoonists do without mouse characters? Mighty Mouse, Speedy Gonzales, Jerry's Tom, The Mickey himself. In a realm where mice sometimes chase cats and keep dogs for pets, only writer Thorton Burgess portrayed them accurately: constantly hunted by every form of predator both great and small, in a never-ending search for food, living anywhere and everywhere.

It is this last ubiquitous quality that gets them into trouble in October when the changing weather creates a need for them to find their way indoors. Like weeds, no one pays them much attention until they appear where they are not wanted.

Last night Susan entered the house and was talking before the door had closed behind her. She told me that she saw a mouse in the garage when she put the car away. She also told me either the mouse goes or she goes. Susan does not like mice.

Actually, I'd known all week we had a garage guest. The few sunflower seeds I had spilled while filling the bird feeder were mysteriously gone the following morning. At some time in the future, perhaps during spring cleaning, we'll move some forgotten item on the back shelf and find a nest of string and leaves and junk in which will be the hulls of the missing sunflower seeds.

Evicting a mouse calls for action. Leaving a note won't help. ("Susan saw you last night. That wasn't too smart. You'd better pack your things and leave.") Those catch-'em-alive devices sound humane, but they don't solve anything. After I caught a mouse in one, I brought the trap outside to release the little guy. He hit the ground and ran back into the garage. Next time, I brought the trap out near the woodpile before letting the mouse out. The following day we had a mouse in the garage again. I didn't check his uniform number, but I felt sure it was the same one. He knew the way.

So I resort to real mousetraps.

House mice are rare in the suburbs. Mostly, I catch white-footed and deer mice (I confess to not being able to tell the difference) and an occasional vole. (Thorton Burgess's *Danny the Meadow Mouse* was actually a vole.) I bait traps with bacon or peanut butter or cheese, but I am not an enthusiastic trapper of mice. Yet I swat flies and mosquitoes with a vengeance. I catch trout to eat. And I hunt, fairly and sportsmanlike, never pretending that bird shooting is any fun for the birds.

Perhaps it is because I hunt that I regret the necessity of my mousetraps. The mouse in my garage is seeking simple survival, doing what is right in nature's world. Emptying a trap into the trash can, I do not think of the fact that mice are, by design, at the low end of the food chain and a necessity for predators every-where. Nor do I reflect on the fact that it is a lucky mouse who lives long enough to see his six-month birthday.

Maybe next year I will try leaving a note. I'll hang it on the barrel where I keep the sunflower seeds, but down low where they can see it. The print will be very tiny, but the message will be clear:

"Be smart. Stay in the woodpile."

* * *

A few years ago, my hometown of Chicopee celebrated its 150th anniversary, and when I visited the local Chamber of Commerce recently, some of the old souvenirs from that celebra-tion were still on display. One of the artifacts was a photomontage taken to commemorate the dedication of the city hall in 1871, with vignettes of the various town landmarks from more than a century ago. Prominently featured was the new city hall, modeled after the Palazzo Vecchio in Florence. There were also photos of several important factories, all long-since gone. The two Romanesque grammar schools in the photo are still in use today. And there was the highly recognizable gothic stone Catholic church on South Street. I studied the old black-and-white picture. The church was different —younger, somehow—but I couldn't quite put my finger on what that difference might be.

On the way home I went out of my way and drove up the hill along South Street. When I got a glimpse of Holy Name Church behind the screening grand old beech tree on the front lawn, it finally dawned on me what had changed. In the old black-and-white photo, there was a recently planted sapling next to the side-walk. In the 130-odd years since its planting, that sapling has grown into one-hundred-foot-tall beech tree, and it has spread just as wide. It has enjoyed the luxury of growing in the open without competition from other trees, and over the years it has become huge and full the way beech trees will if left alone. Its smooth bark fits around the trunk like a too-tight dress on a fat lady, with bulges and sags in unusual places, and the shallow roots have humped-up the sidewalk and taken over the lawn. Like all old beech trees, it is monstrously beautiful.

What had the tree seen in a hundred and thirty years? It was there when trolley cars climbed South Street, and it endured the famous blizzard of 1888. It saw John F. Kennedy drive by when he campaigned for president in 1960, and it stoically suffered count-less school kids scratching their initials in its bark. It was already an old tree when the Elms College was founded right around the corner—it was *The College of Our Lady of the Elms for Women* back then. Things change, but some things endure.

People have an almost universal inability to envision a future (or a past) that is unlike the present. That inability is often demon-strated when they plant trees and shrubs. The crowded, flat-sided yews and boxwoods that populate the foundation plantings here off Main Street are testimony to that failure, as are the trees that overhang the roofs of their owners' homes. As nursery plants, they all begin as tiny, pathetic things that look lost and forlorn when spaced properly. Looking into the future and seeing the size they'll be in ten years is tough to do, and imagining them as mature trees and shrubs is tougher still. Finding the right place for the sapling that someone planted on the lawn of Holy Name Church 130 years ago took more than a little imagination.

On a stop at historic Old Deerfield Village in northern Massachusetts, a visitor almost immediately notices the full and graceful trees that dot the lawns and line the streets. Conspicuous by their absence are utility poles and overhead wires. At Deerfield, in order to preserve the appearance of things as they were before electricity, all the cables have been run underground. The improvement from an arborist's point of view is remarkable. The Holy Name beech was lucky enough to grow in the open space of the church's front lawn. Most other city trees aren't so fortunate. Because of the universality of overhead utility wires, urban trees are hacked and disfigured and made to grow in the shape of wishbones or doughnuts.

Trees outlive us, sometimes by several life spans. As such, they are living connections with the past. There's a horse chestnut tree outside the farmhouse where my father was born in Hazardville, Connecticut. It was there and reportedly producing nuts in 1909 when my grandparents moved in and was there when the gas station down the road was a livery stable. My father can show me where a swing used to hang from a horizontal limb and where the farm horses were tied in its the shade during lunch breaks.

The trees I have planted in the thirty years that I've lived in this house have all grown taller than the roof but are still young trees. The linden in the backyard and the pin oak on the front lawn will still be young trees when I'm gone. I hope I've done them as good a service as did the arborist who planted the single beech at Holy Name Church all those years ago.

* * *

For a scant few days in mid-October, there is a period when the word "fall" actually translates into what's going on. Often there is a bit of rain in the wind gusts, and the wet hurries the leaves down all the faster. Other days might be just as breezy, but this day is so much more dramatic because the wind has something to blow around. At times the effect is the same as being in a snowstorm, with yellow and brown leaves swirling around. Like snowflakes, no two leaves are quite alike, and, again like snowflakes, they're destined to "melt" and be absorbed by the soil.

Most of the seasonal changes that take place in nature are gradual. The two exceptions are the autumn leaf fall and the first snowfall of the year. The changes are untypical in their drama and completeness. The fallen leaves block the storm sewers on the street, and here and there puddles threaten to turn into minor floods. The weather forecast includes the phrase "minor street flooding." By week's end, all the trees will be bare except for the oaks, which are on their own timetable. Wrapped up in October's leaf fall is the old-time farmer's feeling of work done and the close of a season. For a week or so the fallen leaves are like an ocean tide, restlessly swirling and cresting with every breath of wind. But they soon collect in corners and shelters, and begin to mat down. Winter snows will cover the litter, almost like an apology for the mess the summer left behind. But new life will spring from the trash of the old, and only man feels the need to rake up the leaves.

The brevity of the fall season makes our love all the more bittersweet. Autumn is nearly over. November, next up, may still be autumn by the calendar, but New Englanders know winter when they see it. The sound of the wind in the bare treetops hasn't been heard since the buds opened last April. Pumpkins appear on the front steps of the homes just off Main Street, and trick-or-treaters signal the end of another month and another season.

Chapter Nine

THE MEMORY OF THE YEARS

November is berry-bright and firelight-gay, a glittering
night, a crisp blue day, a whispering wind and a handful
of determined fence row asters.

And November is the memory of the years. It is turkey in the
oven, and plum pudding and mince pie and pumpkin and
creamed onions and mashed yellow turnip. It is a feast and
a celebration; but it is also the remembering and the
Thank You, God, and the understanding.

–Hal Borland, *Sundial of the Seasons*

A week before Thanksgiving, there is a serious chill that even
the bright afternoon sunshine can't displace. November is
capable of such dichotomies—deceptively bright sunshine accom-
panied by equally deceptive chilling temperatures. It is the first
wool-shirt day of the season.

At the wood crib, I gather up an armload to bring into the
fireplace. I'm taking maple that was split last winter and some of
the yellow birch that I cut in March. After eight months of seasoning, it should burn well. It should, but until tonight's fire—

the first of the year—I won't know for sure.

Each time I consider the length of time needed to properly season firewood, I recall another armload of maple I once carried to another fireplace. That was thirty-odd years ago when my wife and I were visiting our parish priest to discuss the baptism of our daughter. The rectory of the church was an old mansion that had originally belonged to an industrialist in town. When I admired the stone fireplace, I was invited to bring up some firewood so we could enjoy it properly.

There was a stack of cordwood against the back wall of the cellar, and nobody seemed to know for sure just how long it had been there. The firewood predated the old house's being designated as the parish rectory in 1950, so that woodpile had to be at least twenty-five years old, maybe more. The cellar was dry and airy, and to say the wood was well-seasoned would be an understatement.

After arranging a half-dozen chunks on the grate, I stuffed a crumpled ball of newspaper beneath the wood. I thought we'd need some kindling, but our host lit a match to the newspaper. That brief flare of flame produced enough heat to ignite the eight-inch chunks of split maple, and in just a minute we had a roaring fire.

The maple, of course, had dried to a point where it was nearly explosive. Nobody seasons wood for a quarter century—at least, not on purpose. But if you could, I can guarantee you that you wouldn't need kindling.

Water makes up most of the weight in everything alive, including wood. So it follows that green wood is wet wood. You can't burn it that way. Oh, it'll burn after a fashion—live trees burn in forest fires. But on the hearth, unseasoned wood will smolder and struggle to keep burning, and any heat that's produced just goes to boil off the internal water.

Properly seasoned wood will burn without an excessive amount of generated heat going to evaporate whatever internal water remains. The accepted standard of "dry" is 20 percent moisture content. Since most of us don't have the sort of instrumentation needed to measure such things, we end up guessing. And our guesses are based mostly on time. Right now, my guess is that cordwood split and stacked before the spring thaw will be properly seasoned by late fall. That is, unless I bring in an armload and discover that it isn't.

Some men will tell you three months of drying is enough. Others will swear seasoning needs eighteen months. Scientists have found that wood essentially stops loosing its moisture after a year outside—it's as dry as it's going to get, and any additional moisture losses may be negated by reabsorption. Of course, those scientists weren't doing their research in the dry cellar of Saint Patrick's parish rectory. If that old wood wasn't at zero moisture content, it was pretty close.

There is a missing piece of knowledge needed to answer the question of "how long?" That piece is the amount of moisture the green wood contains. Logically, the woods that will season quickest are those with the lowest moisture content to begin with.

The field guides aren't much help to a woodburner. They'll tell you what the bark of a particular type of tree looks like and how to recognize the leaves and buds, but they're not going to discuss the heat potential and water content of the tree's wood. That would be a bit like *The Birds of North America* describing the table qualities of the Canada goose.

Ash as living wood is fairly dry—it contains only about 35 percent moisture. There is an old woodcutters' motto that says, "Ash green is fit for a queen." And it's true; freshly cut ash will burn nicely, although the motto doesn't mention that properly seasoned ash will make the same queen happier still. Locust at 37 percent moisture finishes a close second to ash, and beech at 38 percent isn't far behind. Those woods will all dry quickly. Cut to length and split and stacked, ash or locust or beech will be ready to burn in just three months or so. Conversely, more than half the weight of freshly cut red oak is water, which serves to explain that wood's reputation for taking a long time to season properly.

Wood left in contact with the ground is prone to rot, so it has to be stacked. A freestanding pile is best because the natural airflow can circulate through it. Wood stacked under shelter or against a wall doesn't get quite as much circulation, and wood covered completely with a tarp is protected from the rain but will get poor air circulation and is likely to decay before it seasons.

As ideal as freestanding woodpiles are to effective seasoning, they have a less-than-endearing habit of falling over. After struggling for years with various methods and systems of stacking wood (none of which were ever stable over three feet high), I finally did it right and built a legitimate wood crib against the side of the garage. I used four-by-four timbers and notched them like Lincoln logs and put a corrugated fiberglass roof over the whole arrangement. It'll hold two full cords and then some. Of course, keeping the seasoned stuff up front and the green wood in the back creates a whole new set of problems, so I still spend as much time handling and restacking as I did back when I had the collapsible stacks in the yard.

For someone concerned mainly with heat, oak—particularly white oak—is prized among northeastern wood burners because it is plentiful and will burn all night without necessitating what's come to be known as the "four o'clock feeding." That is, the restoking of the stove in the middle of the night. Similarly, beech and hard maple would never be turned away by a woodstove operator.

A fireplace operator doesn't care much about heat—most of it is going up the chimney anyway. Instead, he wants to enjoy a bright and lively fire that won't throw sparks and catch his rug on fire. Toward that end, I've found that any of the birches or maples will make an ideal fire on the hearth. White oak, beech, and ash will positively not throw sparks. Just about everything else will, from the occasional innocuous crackler from maple to the Fourthof-July sparkler that is hemlock on the grate.

If you had a pyrometer and could measure the heat of burning wood, you'd find that white oak or hickory burns several hundred degrees hotter than pine or aspen. Oh, they're both hot enough to burn your hand off, but where pine may be burning at fourteen hundred degrees, a similar fire of white oak might be burning at sixteen hundred degrees. People in the know about such things tell me a component of the wood called *lignin* accounts for the difference, although the story from a chemist's standpoint is undoubtedly far more complicated than that.

Knowing that certain woods burn hotter than others, some folks use a chunk of oak or hickory as a backlog on the hearth. Once it gets going, it can help some other woods that seem to have a tough time burning—cherry or locust, for example. Or apple, which burns very aromatically but often needs a little help.

In my own case, where I now burn only in the fireplace and go through just a cord or so each winter, supply is not the problem it used to be when I was heating the whole house with wood and went though a cord every few weeks. My ramblings around the out-of-doors produce enough fallen or discarded trees to keep my woodpile supplied, and it's a rare day when I don't return from a trip with a few logs in the truck.

But I've become selective. Twenty-inch pieces fit best in my fireplace, so that's all I cut. And I only want straight pieces that will split easily—no more crotchy axe-eaters for me. Birch is my favorite, particularly yellow birch. I like easy-splitting ash and beech and any kind of maple, but lately I've been passing up oak and cherry and hickory. I'm becoming fussy, I know. It's nice to be able to afford that luxury.

* * *

On these late autumn days it seems that nature is at rest, awaiting the coming winter. But there's a gray squirrel on the front lawn, busy planting new trees. The process is indirect: squirrels (and chipmunks and blue jays and dozens of other seed hoarders) are busy gathering acorns and stashing them away. Should the squirrel not live to eat all the nuts in his stash—and considering his place on the food chain, that is a distinct possibility—some of those same nuts will sprout in the springtime. Hickories and oaks that grow out of stone walls are living proof of this alternate outcome. In my own yard, oak sprouts mark the forgotten acorns buried by the neighborhood squirrels.

All seeds desperately need to find new ground on which to grow. They parachute or helicopter on the breeze or float away on the flood. They roll downhill or are carried off by the same wind that blows the dust around. Acorns that simply ripen and fall to the ground won't make it—if they were to sprout where they land, they would be growing in the shade of the parent tree. To have any chance for success at all they need to be carried to a new location. Thus, the seeds of the oak evolved as edible nuts to entice animals to unwittingly carry out that relocation. Only a rare few of the multitude will become seedlings. The rest are, by design, squirrel food. It's the original form of chumming, and might seem wasteful to man, for whom efficiency is the key to success. Not so in nature, where the surplus of seed production feeds the world. A single oak can produce ten thousand acorns each year for a hundred years, yet if just one of them grows into a tree, the oak will have fulfilled its natural function of reproducing itself.

The oak is not alone in its excess nor in its reproductive strategy. All of nature's plants have evolved tricks to get their seeds to a new location, and sometimes those strategies involve birds and animals and even you and me. Every fruit, every type of grain, every nut and most vegetables are either seeds or an elaborate form of seed pod, and are part of that "please eat me" reproductive ploy. In the apple's scheme, we are tricked into planting new trees by accepting the lunch hanging from the apple bough. Afterward, we're counted on to be a litterbug and toss away the apple core, which contains the all-important seeds.

The process of sexual reproduction is cutely called "the birds and the bees." The euphemism refers to the idea that the plant kingdom has enlisted the insect world—bees, for the most part—to pollinate its flowers. The birds come into play when it comes to distribution of the seeds. Birds eat seeds, either directly (as they do with sumac) or indirectly (as when they eat a blackberry and swallow a few of the seeds in the bargain.) Some seeds pass through the bird without being digested and end up deposited—complete with a dab of fertilizer—far from the parent plant beneath wherever the bird happened to perch.

Inadvertently, I became a Johnny Appleseed of sorts. There was no bittersweet in my neighborhood—maybe none in the entire city of Chicopee. But a few years ago, I brought home an armload of cuttings for an autumn wreath, which we hung on the front of the garage. The woven vines with their clusters of bright, lacquer-red berries made for a lively and seasonal decoration.

Then birds discovered the wreath.

Within two weeks, the berries were gone. The following spring there was a new variety of vine-like, woody weed appearing in my shrubbery. It was everywhere. I soon noticed incipient bittersweet climbing some of the trees in the woods behind the yard. Bittersweet vines don't take long to become established, and quickly overgrow their host and form dense tangles. I've noticed the neighbors pulling it out of their gardens and foundation plantings. Thus, I became the local Johnny Appleseed of bittersweet. But don't tell the neighbors.

Of all of nature's tricks for seed dispersal, none is more clever than the strategy of the hitchhiker brigade. The clinging seeds are called beggar lice, but stick-tights is a more descriptive name. There are dozens of varieties of weed seeds that come equipped with a means to attach themselves to clothing or to animal fur. One familiar type, known as pitchforks or Spanish needles, comes from a weed that is a relative of the marigold. Beggarweed and the flat little three-cornered tick trefoil are members of the legume family. The worst are the burdocks and cockleburs and sandburs. With good reason, dog owners hate them. They'll tangle themselves in a dog's fur, and will hurt your fingers if you attempt to remove them without gloves.

All beggar lice are passive hitchhikers: we must brush up against the plant for the seeds to attach themselves to our clothing. We unintentionally carry off the hitchhiking weed seed and later pull it off our clothing and, when we throw it away, inadvertently plant the seed in a new location. Knowing that, be careful where you throw those stick-tights you pull off, or you'll have them as lawn weeds next year.

I used to joke and say that stick-tights were nature's Velcro. Then I read that the Englishman who invented Velcro actually studied burdocks under a microscope, and took out a patent on the hook-like barbs that he observed. There really is nothing new under the sun.

* * *

Just as there is sometimes an "Indian summer" after the real summer has departed, there is a second autumn that takes place a few weeks after the sugar maples have shed the last of their leaves. Their colors are the same as those of the earlier version, but in a much more understated way. There are yellows on the hillsides, but they tend to be the tan of a vanilla caramel; the reds are the ruddy reds of freshly broken brick; and the purples are those of cordovan shoes—an old pair, in need of a reapplication of polish. This second autumn is one that celebrates the subtle beauty of the oaks.

In spring, oaks leaf out after most other trees, and they remain green right through mid-October, almost as if they realize that their eventual low-key autumn color would go unnoticed in the dazzle that is a New England autumn. Theirs are the last leaves to turn. Still clothed, they now stand out in the otherwise naked early November woodland, interspersed with groves of evergreens.

White oaks produce a crop of acorns every year, supposedly edible, but I don't know of anyone who's eaten more than one. Red oaks drop acorns each year, too, but theirs take two years to mature, and acorn production tends to run in good-year/bad-year cycles. I know, because every other year I have to rake up the huge crop of acorns that drops onto the back lawn from the red oaks that border the yard.

The oak forests played an important part of the story of the wild turkey's reintroduction to the Northeast. In what may arguably be the most successful program of its kind, wild turkeys were captured elsewhere and then released into the woodlands. With their high metabolic rate, all birds have an ongoing need for large amounts of protein. That's not a problem during the warmer months, but in winter there just aren't enough other food sources for a bird the size of a wild turkey to survive. Turkeys depend on acorns and are largely absent where oaks do not prosper.

The interrelated story of the wild turkey and acorns is closely tied to the history of land management in the Northeast. Although most rural land in the region now seems to be continuous forest, it wasn't always so. From the time the Pilgrims stepped ashore on Plymouth Rock until the mid-1800s, the only land management strategy was the constant reduction of the forest wherever possible. We were, of course, an agricultural society, and farming takes place on cleared land, not forests. Woodlands were cut to create farmland, and the fact that the land beneath the forests was rocky and untillable across much of the Northeast didn't seem to matter. At the time of the Civil War, that ongoing clearing of the forest had been accomplished throughout New York and Pennsylvania and the New England states well up into Maine. The all-consuming need for charcoal during the nineteenth century insured that even second-growth forests were quickly cut, and what forested land remained was largely in the form of farm woodlots.

Turkeys are woodland birds, once abundant, but they disappeared from the Northeast along with the forests. As an illustration of just how complete was the deforestation, the philosopher Henry David Thoreau did not see a wild deer or a beaver during his entire lifetime, which spanned the first half of the nineteenth century. Those animals had disappeared, as did just about every other form of wildlife that needed the eastern forest habitat.

In Massachusetts alone, 85 percent of the land was at one time under intense cultivation. That figure seems an impossible exaggeration until you walk the present-day hills and woodlands and discover that nearly every sylvan acre is laced with stone walls. Those walls—some call them stone fences—climb all but the steepest of hills, edge swamps and bogs, and attest to the fact that farmers' fields existed just about everywhere. Walls delineated yesterday's hay fields and gardens, rye and corn fields. Orchards and pastures were planted where the rocks were too numerous or too huge to be cleared. Stone fences fashioned cattle runs that channeled cows from barns to distant grazing fields. They bordered lanes and figure prominently on old deeds marking the boundaries of a man's land. Unlike those of wood and wire, stone fences were permanent.

There was no "North Forty" on stone-country farms. Out of necessity, fields were small. Even an acre can seem huge when a boulder has to be rolled to its edge. When outdoor writer Frank Woolner wrote of stone walls, he mused, "How many tortuous man-hours went into this chore? How many heart attacks and hernias are built into the vast loops and chains of stone the characterize the countryside of New England?" Anyone who walks those walls and recognizes them for what they are has to wonder the same thing.

Farm life was a continuous cycle of drudgery, and people literally worked themselves to death. Summer, fall, and winter each brought its own particular type of toil, but spring was the time of the hardest work. There was plowing to be done, but first the rocks that the winter had heaved up had to be cleared from the fields.

The West was opening up during the mid- to late nineteenth century. Perhaps it was the first walk through his fields after the snow cleared that finally convinced the stone-country farmer to quit. When a man has cleared rocks from the same fields every spring of his life, he knows that this spring's crop of stones won't be the last. There will be more next spring, and more the spring after that.

If there were no buyers for the place—and frequently there were none for the worn-out hill farms—it was simply abandoned. The Conestoga wagons that rolled westward were manned by those same hale farming families from the Northeast. Ahead were Indians and tornadoes and droughts and sod deeper than a plow could bite, but they pushed on. To a New England stone farmer, the promise of rich flatland with no rocks to clear was lure enough.

Not all the old farms were abandoned. Modern dairy farms and truck gardens still dot the countryside from Maine to Pennsylvania, but they are located in prime farming areas, usually the deep top-soil of river valleys or flatlands. There are no stone walls lining those fields. Even a hundred and fifty years ago these were good farms, where a man could earn a living and grow something other than rocks.

But in the hills, nature quickly reclaimed the abandoned land. The fields grew to gray birch and juniper within a few seasons. Sumac and red cedar followed the weeds into the dooryard. The old lanes grew over and were forgotten as the natural course of forest succession saw hardwoods sprout in the shade of the lesser trees. Woodland animals, which had been gradually displaced since the first fields were cleared centuries before, now returned; ruffed grouse flourished in the second growth, beaver ended their northern exile, and white-tailed deer prospered.

There isn't much to be found of the old farms. Reforestation has completely changed the landscape, and rust and rot and the passing seasons have a way of pulling down the accomplishments of men. Sometimes a gravestone or two remains erect in the woodland, marking what was once a family graveyard. Of the houses and out-buildings, only the foundations remain under the moss and ground pine. And a few woody old lilacs and rose bushes continue to bloom each spring near what used to be the kitchen windows of those farm houses, having outlived the dreams of the farm wives who planted them.

But of all the vestiges of these ancient farms, the most ubiquitous and enduring are the stone fences. They are the memory of the years, the results of a way of life that no longer exists. Like the wear marks and sweat stains on some well-used tool, they have a story.

Oaks, wild turkeys, and stone fences: the three are unified in a house-that-Jack-built sort of correlation—one that requires a bit of history to be fully understood. That relationship illustrates the idea that John Muir first pointed out to us— that whenever one tugs at a single thing in nature, "we find it hitched to everything else in the Universe."

Chapter Ten

GREEN WITH PINE AND BRIGHT WITH BERRY

December will be green with pine and bright
with berry, and it probably will be spangled with
frost and snow as well as tinsel

–Hal Borland, *Sundial of the Seasons*

D ecember shadows lengthen, even at midday, and the play of bright light and deep shade delineate the season like little else can. There's been a definite winter slant to the light for the past several weeks, with the sun hanging low in the southern sky. The sunset has more south than west in it, and the greenish tint that shows along the rim of the horizon after the sun has disappeared is a sure promise of an icy morning tomorrow. Even the twilight is noticeably briefer in December, and darkness swiftly follows the setting sun.

Astronomically, the four seasons are equal in length, but the reality in this part of the world is that spring and fall are just brief interludes between the two long stretches that are winter and summer. December is supposedly the last month of autumn, but that's a technicality, too. The leaves are down and ice has formed on the ponds and autumn is gone for another year. Like it or not, winter is here long before the calendar announces its arrival on December 21.

The summer birds have flown south. Those animals that can hibernate are exercising their option and are sleeping through the winter. The last of the noisy bugs went quiet two months ago. In the stillness of winter, the barren trees and near-total lack of visible wildlife adds up to a sense of desolation. Whenever I see a squirrel in the woods or a crow at the roadside, my heart takes a disproportionate leap of joy. There is a sense of relief to witness proof that something is still alive out there after all.

Against such suspicions, I continually fill the two bird feeders with seed, and in return the local chickadees and goldfinches come to the window and keep me entertained all winter.

A visiting neighbor was fascinated by the attention a downy woodpecker was giving to the suet bag I'd hung outside the kitchen window.

"I've never seen a bird like that," she said. "We don't have any wild birds in our yard."

She lived two houses away, and the supposedly birdless yard she mentioned borders the same woods that mine does. But she couldn't be bothered with a bird feeder or with looking out the window, for that matter. I sent her home with a suet bag and instructions for hanging it, and told her that the trains only run where they've laid down railroad tracks. She thought I was being silly.

Birds hold an age-old fascination for man (even my nonobserving neighbor) not just because they can fly, but because of the myriad variations of color and habits. Other animals—everything from mice to coyotes—hide at the sight of people, but birds go about their daily business in full view of anyone who cares to watch them. They are the most visible of wildlife.

To the casual observer, each chickadee appears identical to the next, as does each titmouse and sparrow, so it's difficult to estimate the total number that visit any feeder. Occasionally, an individual bird takes on an aspect that makes him different from the others— a missing toe, perhaps, or an odd feather. The bookmarked bird appears much less often that I would have imagined, and I'm forced to realize that there are not just a dozen chickadees or titmice visiting my feeder, but perhaps a hundred.

Feeding on the spilled seed below the feeders are birds whose natural habits somehow keep them from landing on the perches. There are juncos with pastel-pink beaks seemingly made of jewelry-quality coral. When I open the cellar door, they fly up from the patio like a gray rag shaken in the wind. Mourning doves walk the patio with mincing tiny steps, and a mated pair of cardinals occasionally visits.

Also on the ground are several varieties of sparrows. Because they flock together in winter, you might count a half-dozen different species in the same flock. Sparrows seem the avian equivalent of mice. They scamper around in corners and small places, gleaning bits of food. The close vision of these seed-eaters must be spectacular, because they make a living finding seeds that, to our eye, aren't even there.

Feeding winter birds might seem an unmitigated kindness, but there is a downside. Right now there is a disease spreading through the house finch population that is being transmitted via bird feeders.

Then there are hawks.

I was seated on the porch steps, taking a break in the winter sunshine after shoveling the new snow off the patio. No sooner had I sat down when a hawk swooped over the fence and picked off a mourning dove that was feeding on spilled seed immediately beneath the bird feeder. The gray blur passed ten feet in front of me and was quickly gone. A couple of floating feathers hung in the air like a three-dimensional punctuation mark where hawk and dove had come together. It wasn't as fast as a lightning strike, but the effect was the same.

The marauder was either a Cooper's or a sharp-shinned hawk. They are essentially identical except for size, and even then the fact that females are considerably larger than males provides an overlap of the species. Both are common accipiters—highly maneuverable woodland hawks that make their living by surprising their prey as they cruise wood margins, road edges, and lately, suburban back-yard bird feeders.

Anyone who attracts winter birds unwittingly concentrates potential hawk food. The nervous way all birds constantly look around while feeding indicates they are aware of the danger. Feeders isolated in the open create easy marks for passing hawks. Better to locate your bird feeder near a shrub or a tree so the song-birds are able to retreat into shelter at the first sign of danger.

In addition to the two tube feeders I keep close to the kitchen window, I hang up a pair of suet bags in the linden tree and have two varieties of woodpeckers in attendance all winter. Chickadees also like the suet. Unfortunately, so do the unwelcome starlings. Blackbirds, some folks call them, although that term could be equally applied to several dozen other species. During the winter speckled featheration gives the starling its name. Later, they'll take on their breeding plumage: black glossed with all the colors of an oil slick and set off by a strikingly yellow bill.

What starlings can't do individually they accomplish in flocks. They are welcome nowhere. Were I inclined to be an animist about birds, I would tell you that the assemblage of starlings perched in the backyard maple, keeping an eye on the suet bag, looks for all the world like a bunch of hoodlums. I've heard a congregation of starlings humorously referred to as a "murmuring"—an apropos term.

If you had to bet on which species of bird are the most numerous, the starling would be a safe wager. They are as plentiful in the city as they are in the remote countryside, and everywhere in between.

Starlings are tough birds. I hold a begrudging admiration for them. They remain through the winter, prospering in a climate that most others choose to abandon. If you scratch hard enough for something good to say about them, it might be pointed out that they are great consumers of grubs and caterpillars during the summer. But in their aggressive competition for nesting holes, starlings are responsible for the decline of several dozen native birds, chief among them the red-headed woodpecker and the bluebird.

There were no starlings in America until 1890, when a Shakespeare buff named Schieffelin released a few dozen in New York City. He wanted the New World to have all of the birds mentioned in Shakespeare's plays. Almost immediately, starlings became a blight on the bird world, and we have been trying to get rid of them ever since. The list of introduced species is nearly as numerous as the reasons for their introduction, but Mr. Schieffelin wins the award for the most stupid introduction of all time. Wherever he is, I hope as his punishment he has to clean up after the starlings. If those birds are as plentiful and as messy as they are here just off Main Street, his punishment is just.

* * *

The leaves are all down now—at least, those that are coming down are already there. Illogically, there are a few oaks and beeches that hang onto some of their leaves right through the winter. Neither tree makes use of the old leaves, and they represent a liability when winter storms load snow and ice on a tree's branches. Yet, in mocking testimony against the obvious, the dried leaves remain on the trees. I've never figured out why, yet I take a small comfort from the paradox.

In the backyard's maple, a paper wasp nest, hidden all summer by the foliage, now stands exposed. It is dormant, but still frightening. Elsewhere, birds' nests are revealed as they begin to fray in the winter wind. Now that the forests are bare, a drive through the

Berkshire Hills reveals a more open landscape. Without greenery or the softening effect of snowfall, the true shape of the land is visible. In the distance, the outline of hills can be traced beneath their hair-like covering of now-naked trees.

We've had a few flurries and a light dusting last evening, but the real snow hasn't arrived yet. In the suburbs, this first sugaring looks like fallout from a spray-paint job and will most likely be gone by evening despite the subfreezing temperatures. Evaporation works even on ice crystals. The storm has blown over and the day has become the sort when the winter-blue sky goes all the way to the horizon.

When I take a walk beyond the back fence, the new snow cover in the woods is marked with the hoofprints of deer. There are several bare ovals where the deer bedded down during the snowfall. Pretending I'm Daniel Boone, I place my hand on one of the beds, feeling for warmth but finding it cold. The few deer that were here during the night could be long gone or, just as likely, standing watching me a hundred yards away. In the woodlands, winter deer are gray, shadowy animals against a gray, shadowy background, and often go unseen until they twitch an ear or flick a tail.

Deer are everywhere. Although people who live just off Main Street doubt so large an animal can live undetected among them, a walk across the new snow reveals their near-universal presence in vacant places and wood margins. With their penchant for eating shrubbery and gardens, suburban deer have become a problem. Their increased numbers have brought an infestation of deer ticks, and deer versus car collisions keep body shops busy. There is very little that the fish-and-wildlife agencies can do to control the expanding deer population, since these suburban deer are safe from hunters, and seem to know it.

Returning, I find where a small animal has crossed my track since I passed. A possum? Maybe the raccoon that has been raiding the trash cans these past few weeks? In the shallow snow the track is unclear, and I follow it for a short while until I catch sight of the footprint maker. The neighbor's orange-and-white cat scampers up a tree at my approach. Daniel Boone is humiliated.

As I'm approaching the gate leading into my yard, I notice that the compost pile has no snow covering it. That fact belies the idea that nothing is happening beneath the surface at this time of year—the internal heat of decomposition has melted the thin snow cover on the pile.

Compost, of course, is highly prized fodder for all gardening and root beds. When ushered properly, vegetable matter can be broken down into compost in the relatively short span of a few months. At least, that's what I'm told. I've never done it. My mulch pile is mostly the summer's grass clippings and the autumn's fallen leaves raked from the lawn. In truth, having a place to dump the clippings and leaves is far more important than any usable compost that might result, so what I've got here behind the backyard fence isn't so much an organized compost pile as this year's trash heap. But there is a formula: so much green matter, so much brown stuff, proportionate amounts of fertilizer and limestone, proper aeration, and turning the pile on a scheduled basis. Gardening magazines can get pretty specific as to the makeup and mechanics of a proper compost pile.

Decomposition needs fuel. I once accepted half a truckload of fresh wood chips to be used as mulch in a flowerbed. The idea was that a layer of mulch several inches thick would keep the weeds from sprouting. The mulch worked—there were no weeds—but the flowers I planted hardly grew. I fertilized, but it did little good. Later, I realized that the wood chips were decomposing and absorbing nitrogen from the fertilizer as fast as I could put it on.

To a lesser extent, the same decay is taking place on the forest floor. By the end of autumn you can't find much left of ash or hickory leaves—they're ready to crumble into dust before they fall off the tree. Maple leaves will decompose in a year or so, but oaks are famous for the persistence of their leathery leaves. My dad favors them as winter mulch for his rose garden because they don't break down. They provide a fluffy blanket for the roses all winter, and can be raked out pretty much intact in the spring.

There are oak trees bordering my yard—all of them the black oak variety of the red oak family. Every year they dump a new three-inch layer of fallen leaves on top of the old. I've lived here thirty years, and the fact that the layer of leaves isn't seven feet deep by now indicates that oak leaves eventually decompose. They just take longer than other foliage.

Right now the fall's oak leaves lie on the surface of the forest floor, and if they've broken down at all in the six or seven weeks since they fell it's not obvious to me. Immediately beneath them are the leaves from the year before, and although all the color has leached out of them, they too appear intact. The only holes in these year-old leaves are those that bugs chewed into them when they were still alive on the tree. Beneath them and fairly well packed down are two-year-old leaves. Here, finally, you can start to see some decomposition. The substance of the leaf between the veins has begun to break away, and although still whole, the leaves are gauze-like and transparent in places. There are still recognizable three-year-old leaves beneath that layer, although at this point the leaf has become brittle, and it is difficult to handle an individual without having it fall apart in your hand. Digging a little deeper, I can find no four-year-old leaves, just pieces and remnants and the detritus that is humus.

The surface of the earth is one big compost pile, constantly renewing the layer of soil that separates the atmosphere from the rock below. The process is one of the many cycles in nature, and has been going on for a long time, but the layer is still remarkably thin. There are a few basic elements that all life depends upon: the sun, the water cycle, the ozone layer, the green miracle that is photosynthesis. On that list has to be the thin mantle of soil that clothes the earth. Without it there is no life.

* * *

Today I'm going out to Ron's farm to cut a Christmas tree. Ron plants his own spruces and firs on land behind his garden. They are grown, tended, and trimmed with the sole intention that they be harvested as Christmas trees. For some people, cutting a plantation-grown rather than a naturally occurring wild tree makes it somehow easier on the conscience when the Christmas tree is thrown out a few weeks from now.

Ron grows white spruce and the wonderfully aromatic balsam fir. The latter's popularity is a function of their soft needles—you don't have to wear work gloves to handle the tree or to hang ornaments. But the commercial harvesting of trees as lumber continues to be an ongoing business all across the Northeast. On highways, self-loading trucks piled high with logs pass each other traveling in opposite directions. Logs head north from the south and east from the west and vice versa. There are sawmills scattered all through the area; you'd think they could get together.

Lumbermen prefer trees from the crowded forest even though they grow more slowly than those in the open. The tree trunks grow long and tall while competing for sunlight, and the wood is nearly free from knots. To be worth anything at all, a timber tree has to be able to produce a knot-free log at least eight feet long with a diameter thirty inches or better.

The East's white pine continues to be valuable—it is much favored for millwork—but other softwoods are almost universally turned into wood pulp. Oak never has been worth much, at least not in the Northeast. It's harvested, but mostly it ends up as low-grade lumber.

On the other hand, certain hardwoods of harvestable size can be worth a great deal, both as lumber and as "peelers" for veneer stock. Lately, sugar maple, white birch, and black cherry are much sought after, and a good tree can translate into several hundred dollars for a landowner.

I spoke to John Seward, who owns an extensive piece of property in Vermont. He recently had a hillside harvested of its tall pines.

"It's amazing that my grandfather used to make a living off this land, and yet what I got last year after cutting that hillside barely paid the taxes."

I was bold enough to ask him how much money that was. He told me that after he split the profit with the logger, his sixteen acres of Vermont pine and hemlock brought in $2200.

"I could have made half again as much, but I waited too long," he said.

Too long? The trees get bigger every year, so unless you have a forest fire, how can you be too late in harvesting?

"I had too many unharvestable trees," he told me. "They're so shallow rooted that big ones are easily blown over, or sometimes the tops break off. The tree's no good after that, and as often as not the one that falls takes down a couple of its neighbors along with it."

So bigger isn't always better. Even trees that are not normally shallow-rooted are susceptible to wind blowdown when they grow on the thin-soil-over-solid-rock situation that exists in much of the Northeast.

Money can be made, but when lumbering is done commercially it's not a neat process. Lumbermen only want the tree trunk, so they leave behind a random tangle of branches and slash, sometimes so much so that a man on foot can't get through. That, and the obscene river of mud that often results from the heavy equipment traffic across the forest floor, is enough to discourage anyone from timbering his land.

At Ron's, we select a small balsam fir. Out in the open it looks tiny, but I know from past experience that any tree taller than me will not fit comfortably under our ceilings once it is mounted in its stand and topped with the Star-of-Bethlehem ornament. The tradition of bringing a live tree indoors is left over from a time when people wore sweaters all winter and drinks served at room temperature needed no ice cubes to keep them cold. Things have changed. In this age of central heating, the sounds of the season that are sleigh bells and carolers also have to include the constant fall of dried evergreen needles in the front parlor.

In among the branches of the little balsam, I notice a tiny bird's nest left over from the previous spring. My first impulse is to remove it, but then I think better of it. The nest will stay and become this Christmas tree's first ornament. If Santa is anything like the fellow I think he is, he'll appreciate that.

* * *

As every school kid learns, the earth is tilted on its axis. As it spins on its daily rotation, it is at a 23½-degree slant to the path of its orbit rather than straight up and down. That tilt means that during the summer our part of the planet leans inward toward the sun, and that posture results in extra long days and a warming of the earth. June enjoys fifteen hours of sunlight in each twenty-four. But the reality of that 23½-degree incline comes home to roost in winter, when the earth leans in the opposite direction. For all of us here in the northern hemisphere, it makes for short days and a low, shallow arc to the sun's path through the daytime sky.

December days are just nine hours long. It is a dark time. When you total the hours of daylight, you find that despite its thirty-one calendar days, December seems to be the shortest month—it has just 285 hours of daylight. (February, with three fewer days, has nearly twelve hours more daylight.) The phenomenon of depression caused by lack of sunlight has long been suspected but only recently proven. It's real. During this dark time of the year, people who work indoors often end up driving to work in the early darkness and then driving home after the sun has gone down. Just the thought of a day without sunshine can put anyone in a melancholy mood.

If December is about darkness, it's also about waiting. The world seems at rest, maybe even dead. The silence of the insects belies the fact that next June's fireflies are waiting out the winter, ready to hatch from eggs and populate the meadow again. So are July's beetles and August's grasshoppers and, unfortunately, May's mosquitoes. Next summer's weeds and wildflowers are similarly waiting in the form of scattered seed, ready to continue the cycle of life.

We spend our lives seeking the truth. We have all become weary of promises and compromises, of spin and interpretation. We are skeptical of anything we can't see for ourselves. Is it no wonder, then, that we return to nature? There are promises in the seed and the shoot, promises that will be kept in June and September. The truth is there in its unarguable certainty. It is elemental.

Hal Borland wrote of the comfort found in living with the land and constantly rediscovering the great assurances of nature. In the dark silence of December it can seem that life has stopped, but there are certainties in the rhythms of the seasons. Anyone who thinks of winter in terms of death should take some measure of comfort from that observation. December time flows by as surely as it does in May. The fallen leaves have already begun to break down and return to the soil. Life hasn't quit; it rests and waits for the spring that it knows is coming.

There are the holidays at month's end, which in their beginnings observed a waiting of another kind. Over time, the holiday itself has grown and evolved into a secular celebration of man's goodness and generosity toward his fellow man. The old signs remain: the tree, the holly, and the wreath, all timeless symbols of the season. Green with pine and bright with berry, earth abides in December, and we along with it. It's a time for waiting and for patience. Only the wind hurries.

Chapter Eleven

THE BEST AND WORST OF WINTER

The cold days and the long nights are ours, the
best and the worst of winter. Long nights and early
evenings, fireplace evenings for long thoughts
and simple comforts....Winter, which drives man
in upon himself and tests his mettle and
his understanding.

–Hal Borland, *Sundial of the Seasons*

I've yet to hear a good explanation as to why some long ago calendar maker decided that the year starts in the middle of winter. As I mentioned earlier, the vernal equinox—that is, the first day of spring —seems a much more appropriate time for a beginning. An argument might be made for the winter solstice, since the days then begin to grow longer after six months of continual abbreviation. But why a bleak winter day with no astrological or astronomical meaning?

One story is that the Romans decreed that the year begin on the day they first saw the thin sickle of the new moon after the winter solstice. But like Easter and Passover and any other event tied to the cycle of the moon, that particular day is difficult to pin down and tends to run all over the calendar from year to year. Why an arbitrary eleven days after the winter solstice?

The reason is one of those facts lost to history. But it's New Year's Day nonetheless, and no one dares make a loud noise this early in the morning out of consideration for neighbors who might be sleeping-off last night's celebration. No one, that is, except the black ducks down on the river.

On this and other winter mornings, if there isn't any wind, I can hear them calling. By their raucous, reedy quacking they're definitely black ducks. They are the would-be state bird of New England, if ever there was such a thing. Like barnyard roosters, they feel a need to sound off at dawn and tell the world that life is good.

Some black ducks migrate, but many more spend the winter on whatever open water they can find here in the northeast. It might be that those wintering on the Chicopee River have moved in here from Labrador or some other point north, but most likely they're local year-round residents. It is anyone's guess why they choose to hang around during the bitterest months of the year when more sensible ducks have retreated to warmer climates.

Black ducks aren't black, although they certainly appear to be when seen sitting on river ice. If you would paint them accurately, you'd use the dark brown color that is burnt umber right out of the tube. Old-time duck hunters used a blowtorch on their cork decoys to produce a nearly black flat finish.

Black ducks are native to the Northeast, and are about as rugged and hearty a duck as there is. They are known in duck-hunting circles for their wariness. But they're not without their problems. Their population is in decline largely because they cross-breed with mallards.

The two species are closely related. A hundred years ago mallards were not found in the Northeast and the black duck population was pretty well isolated. But for reasons unknown, mallards have moved in and the numbers of black ducks have been dropping ever since.

The slight genetic differences that separate the two species are evidently not very persistent because, unlike most crossbreeding, the offspring of a mallard-black cross is fertile. When those mixed offspring breed, nearly all remnants of the black duck disappear and the second generation, for all intents and purposes, become mallards.

There are two informal subsets among black ducks: the fresh water birds and those that stay on salt water. Even on the coast, where there are saltwater bays and inlets mixed in with freshwater ponds and estuaries, it seems black ducks segregate themselves with no apparent intermixing of the two. Those of us who hunt and eat black ducks recognize the distinct difference in table qualities. The diet of saltwater birds makes them less savory than their fresh-water brethren.

Their population might be shrinking, but that fact doesn't seem to bother the ducks on the river this January morning. I can hear their strident calls on the quiet frosty air, and if I close my eyes I can see them rearing back and lifting up off the water to stretch their wings as they prepare for another winter day.

Winter is an introspective season. So long as the sidewalks are shoveled, there is plenty of time to complete indoor projects without the constant haunting reminder that there are a dozen other chores to be done outside. Today, one of my projects is to begin construction on a rig of cork black duck decoys for my nephew.

I start with sheets of processed cork that are four inches thick. I cut and reinforce and shape the cork according to established patterns, and carve heads from white pine that has spent two years seasoning in the garage. I make keels of oak or maple, and melt lead for ballast. Everything is doweled together so that there are no screws to rust away. A coat of spar varnish will seal the decoy, then primer and a final painting with oils. All that to produce a decoy that, in reality, is no more effective than the hollow plastic models that sell for $40 a dozen.

Handmade cork and pine birds similar to those I construct are sometimes offered in sporting goods stores for $200 apiece. Of course they're not intended for use, but to put on a mantelpiece and serve as mementos of the good old days when decoys (and everything else) were made out of something other than plastic.

A good decoy is first a good boat. My designs are always wider than the real ducks they imitate—a boat builder would refer to that quality as "beamy." The boat/decoy will have to be stable in a chop and ride in a convincing manner in both calm and moving water. They should be cartoon-like exaggerations of real ducks; oversized, sometimes greatly so, with identification marks overstated. The final product is painted with none of the subtleties of the live bird.

To the hunter (or decoy buyer) it seems incongruous that these simple caricatures will outdraw other decoys that are made to look exactly like a real duck, yet they will. The disconnect stems from the fact that the hunter examines his decoys at close range and from a ground level perspective. Ducks in flight see things at a distance and from an overhead vantage point. *Trompe l'oeil* painting is fine for winning decoy contests, and might work if the waterfowler was trying to induce ducks to mate with his decoys. In truth, he needs only get their attention and lure them into gun range.

Considering the decoy's place in both American folk art and the long history of waterfowling in America, there is surprisingly little written about them. I know of just few books on the subject, most written by collectors. Many old decoys were simply hand-made tools with an unambiguous function. If they were handsome, it was in a utilitarian sort of way. Carvers developed a style, and expressed their own ideas of beauty while constructing decoys whose sole purpose was to attract ducks. That definition alone puts decoys in the realm of folk art.

In a relatively short number of years this time period will be known as the twilight of the American waterfowler. Society is constantly changing, and the business of killing wild things for sport is becoming socially incorrect. Sales of hunting licenses are down everywhere and fewer and fewer hunters go afield with each passing year. Hunting is in danger of dying out with a whimper rather than a bang. When that happens, decoys—including those I'm beginning today—will become curiosities.

Yet Currier and Ives prints, so much a part of Americana, feature bird dogs and hanging game and hunters in action. Decoys, hunting horns, and the paraphernalia of muzzle-loading weapons is often part of the decoration of inns and restaurants. If I read society's opinion correctly, it seems hunting is okay so long as it took place in the distant past.

On New Year's Day, with the threat of snow in the forecast, I've begun my latest winter project. I'd like to think that I'm continuing an American tradition, albeit with modern tools. Sometimes people are disappointed to discover that I don't start with a jackknife and a hunk of wood with the bark still on it.

For the duck hunter, the decoy is an infinitely patient assistant. These will take some time and patience, but in the introspective season of winter there's plenty of that.

* * *

Holiday cards love to picture winter in New England: glistening snow-covered landscapes under a startlingly clear and cloudless sky, all sunlit and shadowed in cobalt blue. Every winter sees a few days like that, and as lovely as they can be, they are the exception to the rule. The past week was far more typical of the season's theme: each day saw a thin glaze of cold overcast in the sky, made lemon gray by the weak sun struggling through the cloud layer. Shadows were nonexistent. When people move to Florida to escape winter, it's not the Christmas card days they are fleeing, but these protracted stretches of dreariness.

Today the weather is changing, and in the lowering sky there is no sign of the sun. Despite the thickening clouds, the temperature seems to be dropping. Anyone who has lived in the Northeast recognizes the signs. It's about to snow.

We all live in the bottom of an ocean—an ocean of air. And like the seas, this ocean has layers and currents that shift and swirl and are affected by everything from the earth's rotation to seasonal changes in daylight and temperature.

Tides and ocean currents are predictable. If you wanted to, you could find the exact time of the high tide in Wellfleet harbor on any given day in the future. For that matter, you could find out what the water temperature would be on that day and be assured that it wouldn't vary by more than a degree or two.

No such predictability accompanies the weather. Sometimes it seems the weathermen have the toughest job in the world. Here in New England, they attempt to predict the unpredictable. Mark Twain is credited with first saying, "If you don't like the New England weather, just wait a minute." Twain may have said it, but since the Pilgrims stepped ashore on Plymouth Rock, people in the Northeast have been living it.

The ancients accurately plotted the paths of the stars and planets, but had no idea about weather patterns. We have always needed to know what the weather will be, so a number of superstitions evolved. Things as diverse as the width of the bands on wooly bear caterpillars to the activities of groundhogs were somehow thought to portend the severity of the winter. In the same category are the weather predictions written in almanacs. There are people who put their faith in such things, and then there are those of us who just smile.

The legions of television weathermen have a perfect batting average as long as they're talking about what the weather *was;* where they start to falter is in the forecast part of the weather report. It would seem that predicting the weather in this computer age should be easy, but it never is. The recent discovery of the *el Niño* effect in the equatorial waters of the Pacific enables scientists, for the fist time, to predict a season's weather with authority, but even then such forecasts are long on generalities. We can track storms and get a better warning of approaching hurricanes and blizzards, yet beyond that, forecasting remains a game of percentages, and those percentages wear very thin when predictions are made more than two days in advance.

Meteorologists speak of the Bermuda high and the Aleutian and Icelandic lows as if they are geographic fixtures. Those air masses take on the characteristics of the earth's surface over which they formed—ocean air is wet and moderate, Canadian air is dry and cold. New England is at the conjunction of several of those semipermanent air masses, and the constant turf war being waged between them brings unpredictability to our weather. If the Atlantic Maritime Polar air mass is feeling its oats, it might push the Continental Polar air mass back up into Quebec and we'll have our typical wintry gray cloudiness. The reverse brings cold, clear weather. When air from the Gulf of Mexico pushes northward, it dumps moisture into the west-to-east air pattern and the result is a snowstorm.

Most difficult of all to predict is not that it's going to snow, but how much we're going to get. The consistency of falling snow depends on a number of varying factors, and two inches of heavy wet stuff probably represents twice as much volume as six inches of light fluffy snow. Today, depending on which channel I tune to, snowfall predictions range from eight to eighteen inches. The weathermen are hedging their bets, of course, but it's enough to say we're in for the first major storm of the winter.

Farmers and gardeners hope for an early snow cover that will last the winter. There is an insulating quality to snow, one that keeps frozen ground from thawing. Without snow, the alternate freezes and thaws that take place in any Northeastern winter raise havoc with not just road pavement, but anything trying to winter underground— everything from a cover crop of winter rye to my father's delicate rose bushes sleeping away beneath their blanket of oak leaves.

Back when asphalt roads and rubber tires were still inventions of the future, snow was hugely important to transportation. Logs and heavy produce couldn't be moved overland at any other time of the year. Things that couldn't walk for themselves had to be hauled on sleds over snow. Towns had rollers to pack down the snow on roadways, and snow was routinely shoveled *onto* covered bridges so that sleighs could pass.

Urban transportation problems have always been complicated by snow and cold. My mother remembers walls of plowed snow with doorways cut into them lining the streets of Montreal when she was a little girl. When she recently made a winter visit to the places she had gone to school, she was surprised that there was so little snow on the streets. Had she been imagining things? Was there less snow today than back in the 1930s?

No. The difference in Montreal is the difference in all urban centers. There is no place in today's cities where the snow can be pushed, and snow plowing has been replaced by snow removal. It can be a daunting task, one requiring heavy equipment, a fleet of trucks and a place—usually a river—where the snow can be dumped.

Not so here just off Main Street. The snowfall is deep but fairly fluffy. The plow will be by soon, and will push half-a-road's width of snow up onto the curb and tree belt—and onto the end of my newly cleared driveway.

We had a snowless winter a few years ago. Part of me—the part that has to navigate the roads and labor to clear the driveway—was happy about that turn of events. But there's still a little boy inside of me, and that kid, when I was last him, loved the snow.
There is a quiet in winter, particularly in new-fallen snow, that at times can make it seem you're in a small room. The effect can be delightful. The neighborhood looks like an illustration for Clement Clark Moore's Night Before Christmas poem. Before the city plow comes by to shatter the illusion, I'll put on my cross-country skis

and tour the neighborhood and try to remember just what it was that that kid used to like so much about winter.

* * *

Unlike summer, when the day takes it time easing into night after sunset, winter twilight is remarkably brief. Late in the day, yesterday's first winter snowstorm has blown over and left a clear and cloudless sky. The sun has hardly set when darkness gathers. Around the neighborhood the porch lights are on early, as they are all winter.

Even before the daylight fades, Venus emerges from the clear lavender above the sunset. Venus is a planet, of course, but it appears to be the brightest star in the sky. It's only seen for an hour or two at dusk or dawn. For four months or so, it's the "evening star." Then it disappears for a few weeks only to reemerge as the "morning star" for another four-month stretch. The ancients didn't realize that each was a different view of the same object, and had separate names for each incarnation. The explanation of the phenomenon involves the fact that Venus orbits the sun along a path inside our own orbit, so we play a celestial game of now-I-see-you-now-I-don't as the two planets chase each other around the sun.

Venus has moon-like phases that can be observed through a pair of ordinary binoculars. Its brightness in the twilight sky is a function of how close earth and Venus are to each other as we circle the sun together, and right now we must be very close because the evening star is stunningly brilliant.

Minutes after Venus makes its appearance, I can see the first bright stars popping out of the gathering dusk—the square of Pegasus high overhead, and to the southeast Betelgeuse and Rigel and the straight-line trio that is Orion's belt. The sky darkens by rapid degrees and the constellations emerge from the gloaming, and in just a few brief minutes it is night.

The moon is in its last quarter and won't rise until well after midnight, but with yesterday's new snow on the ground it'll hardly be dark under the bright winter stars. So before I head inside, I'll take the dog for a walk in the park at the end of the street. That's excuse enough to get away from the streetlamps and do a little stargazing.

Only the faintest band of twilight remains in the southwest where the sun set a half hour ago, and that fades even as I watch. Orion is easy to spot, more south than east at this time of year. The line of stars that make up the constellation's belt seems to point downward to Sirius, the brightest star in the sky but low on the horizon right now.

In the opposite direction is the equally familiar Big Dipper. Another name for that constellation is Ursa Major, the Great Bear. The legends had it that in winter the Great Bear came down to wash his feet in the frozen lakes of the north. And it makes sense, because the handle of the dipper nearly touches the northern horizon on winter nights. Tracing the stars of the Big Dipper invites a mental plotting of a straight line to find the North Star. Polaris, as it is properly named, is at the end of the handle of the Little Dipper, but the rest of that constellation is made up of fainter stars that seem easier to see when I look slightly away.

Constellations are, of course, the inventions of man. A long time ago somebody looked up in the night sky and played a dot-to-dot game with the stars and imagined the connected points resembled something. The Big Dipper actually could be a contour drawing of a ladle or a long-handled pot. But if inventive souls can see the shape of a queen sitting on her throne in Cassiopeia or a hunter with a raised arm in Orion, such people have far more vivid imaginations than mine. Nevertheless, each of those imaginary pictures is named and formalized in astronomy and astrology to delineate a certain area of the sky.

The stars that make up each constellation can be in vastly different locales in the cosmos and are in no way related to one another.

They're just arbitrary groupings as viewed from earth.

To the north, as proof that the earth is rotating on its axis, the constellations can be seen to rotate around the pole star during the course of a winter's night. Those northern constellations—Draco, Cepheus, Cassiopeia, and the dippers—are always in our night sky regardless of the season. Yet others are visible only at certain times of the year. For a long time I wondered about that. Here's what I finally came up with.

Let's imagine for a moment that our corner of the universe is represented by your kitchen, with the pole star and the Little Dipper painted on the ceiling and the Southern Cross on the floor. The stars of the rest of the cosmos are scattered around on the four walls.

In the middle of the room is our solar system, represented by your round kitchen table. The sun is a lighted candle in the center of the table, and the earth is an orange that rolls around the table's rim.

With the lights off, you can see how the candle illuminates only one side of the orange. The dark side of the orange looks out at the kitchen wall that is away from the candle. That's the night sky as seen from the surface of the earth. The orange travels around the rim of the table just as the earth rotates around the sun. As it moves, its dark side will face first one wall and then another. So it is that we can see only one part of the universe and one bunch of stars in winter. In summer, when the dark side of the earth/orange faces the opposite side of the cosmos/kitchen, we see the stars of summer on the opposite wall.

Although it seems obvious, some things cry out to be stated: Our view of the stars is limited to that part of the universe that we can see while facing away from the sun; that is, at night. Tonight, Orion is a prominent constellation in the January sky, one that everyone recognizes. But you're not going to find him in July. Oh, he's still where he always was, but during summer we face Orion's part of the universe when the sun is in the sky and it's daytime. During the course of the earth's rotation on a summer night, we can glimpse "around the corner" to the stars of the autumn sky off to one side and those of the spring sky off to the other, but Orion and the rest of the winter sky is over there on the kitchen wall on the far side of the sun.

Our orbit around the sun will present different views of the universe, but we live in the Northern Hemisphere—the upper half of the earth. Thus, we can always see the pole star and the constellations around it since they're always "above" us—on the kitchen ceiling—in a part of the sky common to all seasons. Conversely, no matter the season, the stars on the kitchen floor are never seen from our vantage point. You can't see the Big Dipper from Antarctica, and you'll never see the Southern Cross from New England.

The zodiac can be explained by continuing the kitchen analogy. Let's say you have a chair rail along the walls. It represents a horizontal equator all around the room. That chair rail/equator intercepts the twelve constellations that are the zodiac. (Actually there are thirteen, but whoever set up the zodiac wanted to have it agree with the twelve months of the year, so he pretended the constellation Ophiucus wasn't part of the group.) Taurus and Gemini and Aries are over there on the wall by the kitchen sink, and on the opposite wall are Scorpius and Sagittarius and Libra. Scattered along the chair rail of the walls in between are the other constellations of the zodiac; Capricorn, Aquarius, Pisces, Cancer, Leo, and Virgo.

Astrologically speaking, when someone is a Taurus, for example, it means he was born with the sun in that constellation. That person's birthday is in late April or early May, when the earth is on the opposite side of the sun from the constellation Taurus. If you could see the stars during the daytime in that situation, the position of the sun in the sky would be in front of the constellation Taurus. Thus, the sun would be "in" Taurus.

Somehow that, combined with the positions of the planets and the moon at the moment of a person's birth, was all supposed to portend something and influence the future of that particular person. Many people took astrology seriously at one time; some still do. Me, I'll save my superstitions for an occasional knock on wood. It's so much simpler that way.

The line of my footprints in the new snow has reached the far end of the park. The dog runs by, leaving a rooster tail of snow powder in her wake. On January evenings like this we experience the best and the worst of winter. The cold is persistent and the snow brings problems as well as loveliness. But overhead the stars seem closer than at any other time. You get the impression that if you could climb a stepladder, you might reach a couple of them in the cold-clarified and brittle night sky. I whistle to the dog and we start back on our flight through the universe—or so it can seem on a starry winter night in January.

Chapter Twelve

THE TANTRUM BEHIND THE LAUGHTER

Here comes February, a little girl with her first
valentine, a red bow in her wind-blown hair, a
kiss waiting on her lips, a tantrum just back
of her laughter.

–Hal Borland, *Sundial of the Seasons*

A lthough it's still winter, I've been hearing the noisy courtship
of a pair of barred owls in the woods behind the house. Owls
pair off and set up housekeeping in mid-February. There must be a
good answer to the "why" of their nesting at this unlikely time of
year, but I have yet to hear it. Those offered by ornithologists don't
hold a lot of water.

Owls are businesslike birds and will have nothing to do with
the romantic foolishness practiced by other birds who might bring
nest-building materials to a mate in a courtship display. In the no-
nonsense way of owls, they simply take over an old crow's nest
and lay their eggs.

Owls hide during the day and do a good job of it, so those census takers who count birds have a difficult time accurately estimating owl populations. In the Northeast the great horned owl, the barred owl, and the Eastern screech owl are fairly common. I routinely see or hear all of them. Supposedly, we also have short-eared and long-eared owls and Northern saw-whet owls, but I can't vouch for their presence since I've never knowingly seen or heard any of them.

The barred owls in the woods behind the house are probably the most common of the clan. If you could get close to one, you might notice the longitudinally streaked breast that gives this owl its name and see that it has blue rather than yellow eyes. Mostly, though, barred owls are recognized by their *Who-cooks-for-you?* call, complete with the question mark at the end. They're out at dawn and dusk, and they will even hunt during the daylight when they have chicks to feed.

Owls are highly specialized birds, having evolved a set of unique adaptations for night hunting. Their wing feathers feature softened edges, which permit owls to fly in absolute silence. Whenever I've inadvertently flushed one from a tree in the woods, I've been startled not so much by the noise of a large bird taking flight, but by the lack of it. It can be an eerie sensation.

The feathered ear tufts sported by some owls serve no purpose, at least none that people have been able to discern. Their real ears are positioned at different heights on the sides of their head and are concealed beneath their feathers. It is thought that this somehow better helps them triangulate sounds. Owls are famous for their remarkable night vision, but it seems they rely far more on their superb hearing to find prey in the darkness. Their booming hoots are intended to frighten a hiding animal into making noise by shifting its position. It is known that they regularly take prey hidden beneath fallen leaves or under the snow, so their hearing must be extraordinary.

But none of that serves to explain just why they start breeding in mid-February. There must be an owly reason, but for now it eludes me.

* * *

This morning I'm indoors in my studio, working on a watercolor. Elmer Schofield, the American impressionist, wrote of how much he enjoyed the challenge of painting outdoors during the Connecticut winter, but that sort of thing is not for me. When it comes to painting watercolors, water freezes when left standing outdoors at this time of year.

And so do I.

This painting will be a late-winter woodland scene, with sunlight among the maples and the snow striped by long, blue violet shadows. There is a trail going from the foreground off into the woods, and the particular challenge of this painting will be to accurately run the shadows across the contours of the path, which has sunken a foot or so below the surface of the snow.

As reference, I have a couple of sketches and some photos I took last winter in Vermont. I was at Mr. Snow's farm and photographed his sons gathering maple sap. Old-time pictures used to depict sap collection with a sled drawn by a yoke of oxen, but Mr. Snow's family uses snowmobiles, and they appear prominently in several of my reference photos. While I'm not one for portraying the old days just for the sake of romanticism, somehow the snowmobile doesn't fit in this particular watercolor. In my design, I've shown two men tending sap buckets and leaving deep footprints in the snow, but I've left the snowmobile out.

Later in the day I take a drive up Route 23 into the Berkshire Hills. I'm still thinking of the watercolor and find I'm paying particular attention to the maples and their shadows in the bare woodlands. I'm on my way to visit Fred Herder. He taps maple trees on his property and produces a few gallons of syrup each year. I'm going to see just how he does it.

Maple trees clothe the hillsides of New England—in some areas, nearly exclusively so. Those maple-covered hillsides are referred to as "sugerbush" in syrup country. And it lately seems that an integral part of every sugarbush is the elaborate systems of plastic tubing and support wires that are rigged from tree to tree. Seen in the leafless woodland of winter, it always reminds me of some giant electrical grid.

The plastic tubing is maple sugaring gone modern. Increasingly, that system is replacing the picturesque covered tin buckets that for so long were a fixture in the New England winter landscape. Since I'm a painter, I'd be the first to agree with anyone who might say some of the romance of it all has been lost. But while emptying a few buckets each day is no big deal, collecting the sap from hundreds of buckets certainly is—those oxen-drawn sleds in the old paintings weren't there just for effect. The work of gathering sap was arduous, often done far off the road in deep snow. The modern tubing connects the tap of each maple tree to a central collection tank, and enables a sugar farmer to work more efficiently.

I've also seen full buckets of maple sap thrown on the ground because the collectors were late and the sap had "turned," either due to rainwater ingress or from being in the sun too long. Plastic tubing, ugly as it is, avoids that sort of waste.

Here in southern New England, the sap flow usually begins right around Washington's Birthday. A series of relatively warm days and cold nights will stir the winter-dormant trees back to life. Water and dissolved nutrients rise upward from the roots through the outermost, thin layers of wood beneath the bark.

The sap isn't rising in just the maples—a pine or any other tree with a gash in the bark bleeds sap for weeks at this time of year. Once the sap rises, the willows and dogwoods take on lively color in their twigs, and the needles of the pines and hemlocks brighten up from their dark, dull winter colors and seem alive again.

For all its importance, the sap-rise process is not well under-stood. It's uniquely seasonal. You can bore a hole into a tree in the middle of the summer, but nothing will flow out of it. The sap flow stops and starts with changes in the weather, and stops for good shortly after the buds open. Then there is the fact that spiles (taps that collect sap) on the south side of a tree will run first, and those on the north side continue to run when the others have stopped. Nobody seems to know why.

At Fred's, the sugar maples he taps have boles three feet across. They are at least a century old. He only taps two dozen trees and uses old-style tin buckets to collect the sap. His daily rounds emptying fresh sap take him a half hour. "I could tap more trees, but then it would stop being a hobby and start becoming work," he tells me.

We walk the collection route together. The early season sap we gather is remarkably clear and waterlike, with just a hint of maple flavor when I taste it. There are rule-of-thumb guidelines for how many taps a tree will support—one spile for so many inches of diameter—but nobody has ever been able to provide me with an answer as to whether or not you can bleed a tree dry. Fred suspects that any tapping stresses the tree. He errs on the side of caution and won't put more than one spile in any tree regardless of its size.

When it comes to maple sugaring, Fred is in every way an amateur. But he's also a retired chemist. He knows more about the chemistry of the sugaring process than most laymen even suspect. His answers to my questions have a decidedly scientific bent.

Inside, he has several large kettles of sap on the woodstove. They don't seem to be boiling, and I ask why.

"Right now I'm just heating the sap to get a head start on evaporating off some of the water," He tells me. "It starts out as 2 or 3 percent sugar in raw sap, and has to be reduced until there's 67 percent in the finished product. That's a lot of water to be evaporated off.

"At the end of the boiling process, you have to pay close attention. There is an exact stopping point when the syrup is done. If you leave even slightly too much water in the syrup, mold is liable to appear on the surface while it's in storage. And if you boil off too much water, it'll form solid sugar crystals when it's allowed to stand. You've got to hit it just right."

"How do you know when it's just right?" I ask.

"The old-time farmers could tell just by the look of the foam. I use a refractometer that measures the amount of suspended solids in the liquid. Another way to check involves watching the exact boiling temperature. When the syrup is ready, its boiling point will be seven degrees higher than when the sap was raw.

"Cooking the sap—that is, boiling it—is an essential part of the process. It's more than just evaporating the water. As the sap is cooked it shifts upward in pH as the sugars change from sucrose to more complex forms. There are actually several reactions taking place. And the microbes contained in the sap are killed in the boiling process."

"Microbes?"

"There are living microbes that occur naturally in all sap," Fred says, answering my unspoken question. "Today's sap is clear because there aren't many bugs in it this early in the season. Their numbers increase continually as the season warms up. But all sap contains microbes. They die in the boiling process and color the finished syrup. The early season sap with few microbes produces clear pale amber syrup—Grade-A Fancy, they call it. As the season progresses, results become increasingly darker. More dead microbes mean darker syrup, so much so that the stuff that's made from the cloudy, end-of-the-season sap is very dark brown, nearly opaque. It's called "buddy syrup" because it's made from sap that was gathered after the buds started to open."

"So there's nothing a farmer can do to control the color of the syrup he produces?"

"Not really," Fred admits. "You can't produce light amber syrup from late season sap no matter what you do. The high count of dead microbes is going to color and darken the syrup. They also seem to add more maple flavor." He pauses for a moment, then laughs. "Maybe dead microbes taste like maple syrup, and the sap has no flavor of its own at all! Wouldn't that be something? But it's true that the expensive early-season stuff looks nice but doesn't have the rich maple taste that the darker syrup has."

As I'm leaving, Fred presents me with a Mason jar of this year's run. It's the expensive stuff, remarkably transparent, light and delicate of flavor. It is homemade syrup, a taste of wild New England made in much the same manner as when Indians first showed the Pilgrims how to boil down maple sap. For much of the intervening three hundrred and fifty years, maple syrup might have been the only source of sugar in a country family's diet and one of the few money crops a Northeastern farm might produce.

The sun has been battling the clouds all day, trying to break through. Unfortunately, the clouds are winning. As I leave Fred's driveway, the sky has a flinty look that promises snow. If the weathermen are right, we're in for several inches of new powder this evening. It is still February, after all.

Ah, but the sap is running. Winter isn't over, but if the buckets are hung in the sugarbush the end is certainly in sight.

* * *

There is a "tired" part of winter when the damage of the season is everywhere, yet it is not time to begin spring-cleaning. Between storms, the bare roads carry a full winter's accumulation of sand that the city has spread when conditions were icy, and they now appear filthy and unkempt. The snowbanks, despite the subfreezing weather, have shrunk in on themselves. What had once been so much whiteness is now a dingy brownish gray. Windblown litter, both natural and manmade, clutters the landscape. We end up actually wishing for another snowstorm to cover it all again. Snow, it seems, is nature's form of apology for the necessity of a bleak landscape through the winter months.

Technically, February is still winter, but each day of this month brings three minutes more daylight than the one before. Three minutes may not seem like much, but by the end of the month the sun is up forty minutes earlier and sets a half hour later. February 20, sixty-one days after the winter solstice, and October 20, sixty-one days before the solstice, each have exactly the same amount of daylight. But there is the inertia factor of seasonal weather to be dealt with: October 20 is still sweatshirt weather, and during the day you would expect to be outside without a jacket. But even if February 20 is a seasonally mild day, you'll still need your winter coat. And it could easily bring a roaring blizzard and subfreezing temperatures.

Then there's the killer wind. Cold air is heavier and more dense that warm air, and a February wind might pack as much as 25 percent more force than a hot summer wind of the same speed. The wind will force its way into even the best insulated of homes. The persistent wind finds cracks and gaps, and indoors we all feel a draft in February.

Outdoors, plants that somehow made it through the bitter months of December and January now succumb to February's killer wind. More than the spectacular low temperatures of the dead of winter, more than coating ice storms or deep snow, it's the wind that kills off young trees and bushes. It shows up as "winter burn" on evergreens and as dead branches and buds on dogwoods and rhododendrons.

It's all February's fault. With the lengthening days, plants start to quicken and make the first stirrings of life. As the sap rises in trees and shrubs, February's killer wind will steal a plant's moisture right through its bark and freeze its rejuvenating buds and capillaries. Some plants are tougher than others. Fred Herder's maple trees laugh at February's wind, but some of my father's carefully pampered hybrid tea roses never come out of dormancy. If they're going to die, it'll be on a windy day in February.

Nursery houses and seed catalogs routinely print maps of the various growing zones in the United States. They're based on length of the growing season and severity of winter weather. Here in southern New England we're on the cusp of the northern limit for flowering dogwoods and azaleas and magnolia trees. They are tender and easily damaged by a severe winter, and the zone charts warn against their cultivation.

But one of the challenges of growing anything is to make it prosper somewhere where it's not supposed to. As a result, New Englanders plant flowering dogwoods and azaleas and magnolias, and if the winter hasn't been too severe they will blossom profusely in the springtime. At such times, nurseries can't keep them in stock.

But in the wake of the sort of real New England winter that we seem to experience every few years, the magnolias and dogwoods and azaleas that are still alive are spotty at best. In those years, they can't compete with the hardy native mountain laurel and flowering crabs when blossom time arrives.

The problem with those tender shrubs is not that they don't go dormant for the winter, but that they don't become dormant enough. When the days grow noticeably longer in February, those southern shrubs think they're back in Savanna and let down their guard.

My personal favorite too-tender-for-New-England shrub is English holly. There are male and female plants, and you'd better have one of each if you expect to cut sprigs of red-berried holly at Christmas. As is the case with so many other tender shrubs, this part of the world is right on the cusp of the holly's acceptable growing area.

Knowing what I was up against, I planted my holly bushes in the crook where the porch meets the house. The corner faces north, so the bushes don't get a lot of sunlight, but they don't need much. They get snow piled on them all through the winter, but they don't seem to mind. My English holly has prospered for thirty years, and all because the sheltered corner provides them protection from February's killer wind.

In the early twilight, as I gather firewood from the crib, the snow that seemed eminent when I left Fred's finally begins falling. It becomes noticeably brighter as the new snow accumulates on top of the remains of last week's blizzard. The big flakes swirl like moths around the porch light. Here just off Main Street, we keep hoping that each new snowfall will be the winter's last. Like everyone else, I'm ready for the end of winter. Once February is over, we still have to endure the purgatory that is March. No matter what the groundhog may have portended last week, the promise of April is a long six weeks away. In February, we can hear the distant laughter of spring, but winter is about to throw another tantrum. It can be discouraging.

Then, from out of the darkness behind the house comes the paired hooting of the nesting owls in the back woods. I shut off the light and stand for a moment, listening to their booming calls and answers in the cold night air. Owls are supposed to be wise. If they have faith that spring is coming, so should I.

Chapter Thirteen

THE PROBLEM CHILD

March is the gardener impatient to garden; it is
the winter-weary sun seeker impatient for a case of
spring fever. March is February with a smile and
April with a sniffle. March is a problem child
with a twinkle in its eye

–Hal Borland, *Sundial of the Seasons*

S pring snow.
Those two words bring up haunting and dreamy images of an overlap of the seasons, pleasant scenes of gentle vernal snowfalls on greening shoots. The snow is temporary at best, and it is a reminder that although spring is nearly here, winter has not completely given up the ghost.

It all sounds very romantic—and probably is—except in spring when it's snowing. Then the people getting snowed upon hate those two words just as turkeys hate Thanksgiving.

We had such a spring snowstorm during the night. The weathermen all warned of the approaching storm, so it was no surprise, but that didn't alter the fact that everyone was ticked off about it.

We are all "winter-weary," to use Hal Borland's term. The few warm days we experienced in early March served only to taunt us. During the spell of mild weather, people had already begun raking out their lawns and sweeping winter sand from the driveway with all the eagerness of folks propelled by a premature case of spring fever. I was out raking with everyone else, so I'll plead guilty there. But a few of the neighbors did something truly foolish: they took their winter woolens to the dry cleaner so they could be put away for the season. We all wanted to believe that spring had arrived, but the reality is that in the first week of March there has to be more cold weather ahead.

After the city plow went by, I went to clear the wall of snow thrown up at the end of the driveway. Several of my neighbors were doing the same. Usually they call out to one another and joke about the weather, but up and down the street the snow shovelers were working off their own private anger. Winters that go into extra innings leave everybody grumpy. Maybe the worst of it is that there's nobody to complain to or blame. No one, that is, except ourselves for permitting our hopes to rise.

We give the month of March its bad rap because we are so impatient. The month stands undecided between the seasons and is associated with craziness, as in "March Hare" and "March Madness," and with such extremes as "In like a lion, out like a lamb." With the coming of March we watch for signs of spring, then celebrate them as if that celebration will stave off the inevitable return to winter. Daylight lengthens, crocuses pop up, painted shamrocks appear in store windows and on the asphalt of Holyoke's streets where the Saint Patrick's Day parade will take place. In the marshes the skunk cabbage sends up its strange, maroon-hooded blossoms, sometimes poking through the last of the ice.

In our impatience, a scene on the evening news tortures us: a television reporter stands outside the White House, and the lawn is Kelly green, and forsythia is blooming in the background. It all seems like a mirage. Five hundred miles to the south, spring is fully underway, but here the city sand truck just rumbled by out on the snow-packed street.

Springtime seems to travel northward at about one hundred twenty miles a week. That is, if a nor'easter doesn't roar in and push it back a week or two. It also seems to climb hills at about one hundred feet of elevation each day. Driving along Route 91 through the river gap in the Holyoke range, you can look up the side of the mountain and see spring advancing. Sometimes, when the early blossoms are open on the red maples along the bottom of the hills, a couple of hundred feet up the trees are still winter-dormant.

We know for certain that although there may still be snow on the ground and frost in the air, spring is on its way north. We know, too, that a March snowfall can't last the way a January snow can, and that the death grip of winter has been broken. It's a time for the sort of patience needed with a problem child. That one word, patience, has to be the motto of March—or rather, of those who must endure it.

* * *

So here we are, back where we began, at the vernal equinox. Those who calculate such things inform us that spring will begin at 7:33 tomorrow morning. Another new year will have started, or will it?

When I was a little boy, my father had a habit that inadvertently shaped my outlook about this sort of thing. On Saturdays, perhaps just to give my mother a day away from the children, Dad would sometimes take us to the movies. Back then a matinee consisted of a cartoon or two, the previews, and not one but two features.

My father wasn't much for paying attention to the published start times at theaters. As often as not, we'd arrive at the movie house and sit down in the middle of one of the two features. Then we'd watch the cartoons and the previews and the second movie.

When the first movie started again, we'd watch it up until the part where we came in, then my father would herd us out of the theater and back to the car.

My dad's this-is-where-we-came-in nonschedule used to gall my brothers. They claimed it ruined the endings of the movies we'd see. In retrospect, those Westerns and comedies back during the 1950s always had conventional story lines, and even the mysteries were fairly predictable. Sometimes it was fun to put a movie plot together out of two disconnected halves. After a while, I came to agree with my dad's way of seeing things. The whole business of going to the movies became a continuous cycle, and it didn't really matter at which point in the loop we came in.

The same theory applies to nature—nothing ever begins or ends. It's all one continuous cycle: the weather, the seasons, the tides, the phases of the moon, everything right down to life itself. As surely as each wanes, the cycle will wax it full once again. There is a continuity in the blossom and the seed, in the dormant bulb, in the cry of a newborn. Here, at the vernal equinox, you need only look at the swelling bud at the bare branch tip to realize that the year keeps flowing, like an unending helix or Möbius strip made of calendar pages taped end to end.

The cycles go on and time slips away, and, although we often wish it otherwise, we can't do a thing about it. James Taylor wrote a song on the subject that I've always liked. It proclaims, "The secret of life is enjoying the passage of time."

In winter, we wish the time would fly by and it was spring, then we wish the lilacs wouldn't fade so quickly. We look forward to autumn, then find it's too quickly behind us. Right now we're coming up on snow melt and mud season, a time people might want to wish away if they could. I spent huge chunks of time away from my home and family during the years when I went to sea, so I know a thing or two about wishing your life away. Mud season won't be here long. We know those things because the crank keeps turning and time slips by, and it doesn't matter if that slipping takes place in mid-March or early June.

The seasons change and the cycle goes on, and the secret of life—if there is such a secret—is enjoying the time as it inevitably passes.

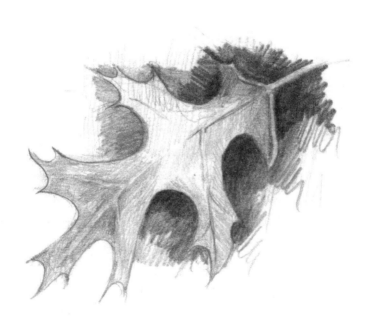